#15114
$30.99

THEY ALWAYS SAID
I WOULD MARRY A WHITE GIRL

Coming to Grips with Race in America

Robert M. Moore III

Hamilton Books
A member of
The Rowman & Littlefield Publishing Group
Lanham · Boulder · New York · Toronto · Plymouth, UK

Copyright © 2007 by
Hamilton Books
4501 Forbes Boulevard
Suite 200
Lanham, Maryland 20706
Hamilton Books Acquisitions Department (301) 459-3366

Estover Road
Plymouth PL6 7PY
United Kingdom

Library of Congress Control Number: 2007922311
ISBN-13: 978-0-7618-3727-5 (paperback : alk. paper)
ISBN-10: 0-7618-3727-2 (paperback : alk. paper)

Dedication

This book is dedicated to the many students over the years who have allowed me to be their teacher.

Contents

v

Preface

I wonder how many of my former classmates ever questioned why there had been no other African Americans in their classrooms or in their neighborhoods other than me. Did they even notice? Back then, did I even notice? What do my children think about their school and neighborhood? Do they notice that all of their friends are white?

Robert M. Moore III; Frostburg, Maryland; October, 2006

I

Straddling the Fence

Chapter One
Assimilation

In my youth, during the 1960's, there were instances when I was reluctant to point out to my classmates, all of whom were white, that I was indeed African American. There seemed to be an imaginary wall or boundary between us. I do not remember intentionally trying to pass for white, although there were times when I just didn't speak up with a loud voice as to who I was.

Although, my skin was quite fair, I would not have chosen to be identified as "mixed," not only because my parents, who also have fair skin did not claim to be mixed, but because that category did not exist at that time. I may have wanted to be white so that I could fit in with my friends, but my classmates *knew* that I was African American.

I often felt I harbored from my friends a secret, a mark or stain, one that my friends and I just didn't discuss for fear of embarrassing me. To be white was right. To be something else other than white meant to attract unwanted and unneeded attention. To be mixed at that time was to be racially lost, without a home base, a "people."

To feel racially the same as one of my classmates didn't seem possible regardless of how friendly or intimate I became – the wall seemed impenetrable.[1] It was vital that I be able to identify with two seemingly opposite camps. But, it was not a two-way street. My friends did not have to try and understand what it meant to be African American. In a sense I was living in their neighborhood, not only because my family was the only African American family, but at this time African Americans were still not considered by many to be equal to whites. I was an outsider.

I did not seek to intentionally develop two identities. It was not deliberate on my part. Because I could see both *sides* I felt very unique. I was one of the few

3

African Americans in the 1960's, so it felt, being raised in an all-white suburb, a time when many African Americans were living within the boundaries of urban America.

My classmates knew I was African American not only because word had spread that an African American child, the first, was now going to school with them, but also because I did not physically look the same as they did, my hair was different. I was close in appearance but not close enough. I had broken an imaginary color line. I was the first and only African American in my elementary school. My lightness of color did not protect me from being treated or feeling different.

There were many days in elementary school, during some sort of school project, when I would emphasize loudly that my grandmother had an Irish mother and a Scottish father. Ironically, I never claimed that she was white and neither did she. Did I vehemently expose these linkages to Europe because I was proud of my heritage? Or, did I have a strong sense of feeling different, feeling stigmatized and thus I wanted to indicate my common white heritage to my classmates, as if to say "I am you," to compensate for the negative images so strongly associated at that time with African Americans by whites and even by some African Americans? I don't know.

In fact I remained quite reticent about my racial identity throughout most of my youth when in school or in my neighborhood, although deep down I knew who I was. I didn't know of any negative images associated with being white at that time but I knew of too many associated with being African American.

I was raised in Upper Darby, a suburb of West Philadelphia. I knew what it was like to feel psychologically wedged between two races and to feel both black and white. I was proud to be African American but was unable to express to my classmates at that time any positive acclamations.[*] The following quote by Adrian Piper, an artist, is significant.

> A benefit and a disadvantage of looking **white** is that most people treat you as though you were **white**. And so, because of how you've been treated, you come to expect this sort of treatment, not, perhaps, realizing that you're being treated this way because people think you're **white**, but falsely supposing, rather, that you're being treated this way because people think you are a valuable person. So, for example, you come to expect a certain level of respect, a certain degree of attention to your voice and opinions, certain liberties of action and self-expression to which you falsely suppose yourself to be entitled because your voice, your opinion, and your conduct are valuable in themselves.[2]

---

[*] See DuBois, "The Souls of Black Folk," (1996). His work on the "veil" or double consciousness is important here.

When James Brown's song came out in the mid to late sixties with the lyrics, "Say It Loud - I'm Black and I'm Proud (Part 1)," I felt like a door had been created and opened that led to a space where my positive feelings of being African American were finally being expressed in some sort of public forum. A forum that I could hear and my classmates could as well. Even though radio stations at that time always identified James Brown, the Supremes and others as soul artists, code for African American and not white. I had also reached an age when, as Mead had written, my generalized other, being able to consider events and information beyond the immediacy, became important to my development.[3]

My parents were the first African Americans to move into the neighborhood of Hilldale. They moved there in 1958 a year after I was born. We were welcomed by some. Others were not so nice. Someone went as far as to send an anonymous letter asking us to leave. The neighborhood is still upper-middle class today but now with a sprinkling of African American families. My parents still live there. Many of the families in Upper Darby other than in the area where I was raised were working class white families.

My sister, three years younger, and I attended Primos Elementary and Beverly Hills Junior High School (not to be confused with the famous city in California with the same name), both located in Upper Darby. She, after Beverly Hills, attended Upper Darby High School. I instead left the public school system and attended a private school, Friends' Central, located in Montgomery County, a wealthy suburb that bordered Philadelphia on City Line Avenue.

There was an African American girl a few years younger than my sister who later attended Primos. Our elementary school was one of several that fed into Beverly Hills. In junior high, out of nearly 1500 students, there were only two other African American students who attended when I did, although I did not know them very well.

My Children

Today my children can identify as biracial if they wish not only because their mother is white, but because more Americans today accept a biracial identity compared to a generation ago.* It is unclear whether or not the existence of a biracial identity signifies a softening or even an eventual doing away of racial

---

* Early in the 1990's, a coalition of mixed-race individuals and advocacy groups from across the nation lobbied the Office of Management and Budget (OMB) for the addition of a multiracial category to the 2000 census. The request was not denied outright....As a compromise, the 2000 census enabled individuals to check more than one racial category if they desired...Support for the multiracial initiative was led by grassroots organizations such as Project RACE and the Association of MultiEthnic Americans. Rockquemore and Brunsma, *Beyond Black*, 2002.

categories in America. It does however indicate that two sides, one black and one white, still exist.

My parents did provide access to an alternative community that compensated for the sense of social difference I felt from my classmates. My father had three brothers and a sister, all of whom had children. His brothers lived in Philadelphia. His sister lived in a nearby suburb where she too had broken the color line in her immediate neighborhood.

My sister and I spent countless hours visiting our cousins and vice versa. We celebrated birthdays together, went to see the Phillies in North Philadelphia at Connie Mack stadium and the Eagles in West Philadelphia at Franklin Field. At Christmas my father and I made the rounds to drop off and receive gifts at their houses.

In 1953, right after my parents were married and living in one of the very few large apartment complexes in Philadelphia that permitted African American tenants, the Flamingo at Broad and Girard, my dad and about eight of his boyhood male friends, all African American and from West Philadelphia, formed a club. They named their club the West Philadelphians.* The club enabled my father and his boyhood friends to remain in touch with each other. They met monthly and collected dues.

The West Philadelphians were like an extended family to me: they were my play uncles, their wives my aunts and their children were treated and felt like first cousins. Those bonds still exist today even though I am near fifty years of age. The West Philadelphians also served as a nexus of continued contact with other boyhood acquaintances my father had while growing up in Philadelphia.

They held an annual New Year's Eve party. In my youth the party was often at my parents' house. As a child I remember thinking about what the neighbors may have thought on New Year's Eve when thirty or so cars were parked up and down our road, on lawns and in the small orchid across from our house. Most of the people in the cars were African American. As I got older the event was held at a hall in Lansdowne, about a mile away, and featured an incredible multi-piece jazz band.

Most who attended the annual New Year's Eve event were African American but there were whites as well. African Americans who attended worked in various occupations and professions that included: a family court judge, a deputy police commissioner, an administrative court clerk, a school principal, a bar owner, a gas station owner (one of the very few African Americans in the 1960's to own a brand-name filling station), a music teacher, an accountant, a fireman, a funeral home owner, a reading teacher specialist, a couple doctors, a professor, a psychologist and more. Many had served in the military during World War II. Among the West Philadelphians and their wives the following universities and colleges were attended for both undergraduate and professional

---

* This is a fictitious name. I have chosen to rename the club.

degrees: Penn State, Temple, Hunter, Bryn Mawr, West Chester, Lincoln, Howard (quite a few), University of Pennsylvania and more. The following were attended by their children: Temple, Michigan, Spelman, Franklin and Marshall, Union, Hampton, Wharton, West Virginia State, Johnson C. Smith, Widener, Tuskegee and more. Some of the West Philadelphians were members of African American fraternities and sororities. Some West Philadelphians, as well as their wives, belonged to other clubs as well. Many of these clubs were started in the 1940's because of the exclusion from white clubs. One member of the West Philadelphians was a Tuskegee Airman, the now famous group of African American pilots who flew in World War II.

In the 1950's, dating across racial lines was severely discouraged.[4] Physical harm could follow for those who transgressed the color line. It didn't matter what shade you were or how straight your hair was, people *knew* who was *Colored* and who wasn't and the two did not romantically mix, at least not in public. Some interracial couples left the country rather than face possible social hardships in America.[5]

A couple West Philadelphians after marriage, my father included, bought their first house in West Philadelphia near where they were raised. They then moved to other sections of the city where there was more space. Sociologists describe this time period during the 50's and 60's as one of "white flight" from urban America to the new and expanding suburbs. Manufacturing jobs had been drying up in the cities and middle class jobs were increasing outside of urban America.[6]

Not only were whites chasing the new American dream of a house in the suburbs, African Americans were as well. Based on the experiences of my father and some of his boyhood friends, African Americans were moving away from the neighborhoods where they were raised. A couple of the West Philadelphians moved to neighborhoods on the periphery of Philadelphia but still within the city boundaries such as Germantown and Mount Airy. The future for African Americans, who moved including my father, was still dependent on ties to Philadelphia for employment, family and social life.[*] My parents in 1958 moved to the heart of a completely white suburb, a suburb that did not embrace their arrival. One West Philadelphian moved to a suburb called Yeadon where there were already numerous middle and upper class African American families.[†]

Although my parents had created an African American community for me, at that time, a sense of pride and positive self-esteem needed to counter the then

---

[*] See DuBois' account of an earlier migration by African Americans near the beginning of the 20th century, to Philadelphia and the accompanying settlement patterns. The migration was not as great in number as the one after World War II. It culminated in a heightened awareness of African American achievements, for example, the Harlem Renaissance in New York. DuBois *The Philadelphia Negro*, 1973.
[†] Yeadon was not completely African American. My mother's mother, who was white, and other whites, lived there as well.

prevailing negative images of African Americans held by whites, was tougher for me to affirm than it was for my parents. I lived in an all white community and most of my time was spent there. My parents had had substantial contact with other African Americans where they were raised. They also had contact with whites.[7]

My mother grew up in Harlem in the 1930's and 1940's, a Harlem not as racially segregated as the Harlem of today.[8] Although my mother's mother was white and her father was black, both born in Jamaica, my mother never saw herself as a mixed-race person. Even today, it is not a term that she would embrace to describe herself. I do not believe that she would have wanted to be considered biracial and few in her generation would have permitted her to see herself that way, just as no one in my generation in the 1960's, at least very few, seriously entertained such a notion for me. My very light skin, when I was growing up, still meant only one thing, that I could be affiliated with the "n" word.[*]

I absorbed and soaked up the values espoused by my white classmates.[†] Their stories of their ancestors, who voluntary immigrated to America, worked hard and moved up the class ladder, became my story. How was I to tell them that most African Americans did not voluntarily arrive in America? How was I to take pride in this information? Their alienation from African Americans in a very real sense became my alienation as well.

The majority of my classmates were the first generation of descendents of white ethnics to be born in the suburbs.[‡] Some of their parents overtly expressed a dislike and even a disdain for me when I was near them. Among those I played with where I grew up, it was usually the fathers who showed overt disapproval of who I was. Mothers tended to be much more tolerant and some even seemed oblivious to my race and accepted me as a person.

Many of my classmates' parents, as was the case with my parents, were born and raised in Philadelphia and ironically probably had experienced more contact with African Americans than their children, or me. Moyer, a sociologist, wrote in her dissertation about the following situation:

> More recently, as blacks moved into the northeastern cities, including Philadelphia, in the late 1940's and 1950's, Irish- and Italian-American families moved out of Philadelphia into the ring suburbs, including Upper Darby, to establish a home there.[9]

---

[*] I only mean to imply here that I was seen as African American.

[†] In the mid to late 60's African Americans were called Colored or Black.

[‡] Sociologically white ethnics were groups from Southern and Eastern Europe that included Southern Italians, Poles, Hungarians, and more.

In the early years of Dick Clark's "American Bandstand" television program, broadcast from West Philadelphia, white and African American teenagers lined up together waiting to get into the show to dance, although to dance only with members of the same race.

Years later in the 1980's I remember routinely taking the "El" (elevated subway) from West Philadelphia, where I briefly lived after college, to downtown Philadelphia. I routinely noticed what was left of the letters that spelled "American Bandstand" that dangled on the marquee on the front of a building where the show had aired. West Philadelphia by the 1960's had become predominantly African American with only a sprinkling of white businesses that remained to suggest that racially the area had been quite different only a generation earlier before "white flight" to the suburbs had occurred.

"American Bandstand" continued for a number of years after leaving Philadelphia in 1964 for Los Angeles. It represented the beginning of a new era. The younger generation was beginning to coalesce and eventually would rebel against the traditional values espoused by their working class parents who were moving to the suburbs. In the suburbs, the youth, particularly in the 1960's openly indulged in social experimentation that is considered today quite routine by many: premarital sex, cohabitation before marriage, drugs and more.

Although my classmates would grow up to be more socially liberal on some issues than their parents, contact with African Americans was infrequent at this time in their schools and neighborhoods. Negative images garnered from the media and stereotypes that lingered about African Americans were harder to combat because of a lack of contact.

Classmates, with whom I had daily interaction, became friends.[*] Although I may have been an ambassador, someone who was racially "new" to my classmates, my contact with whites in my suburb did not alter the overall impression some may have had about African Americans. I was only one person. They were socially more liberal in a number of ways compared to the previous generation, but they still had little exposure to ideas or situations that could have created new or better impressions of African Americans.

In fact their isolation from African Americans may have created even more impenetrable images and negative stereotypes and thus a stronger wall or boundary between the two groups may have existed during this time when the suburbs were rapidly being built than had existed in previous generations. Multicultural practices were just getting started. Given the emphasis placed on assimilation of minorities to the social characteristics of the majority, multicultural movements may have felt more of a threat to many whites in the suburbs at that time rather than a source of comfort. Curiously, an emphasis on multiculturalism occurred at the same time as residential segregation deepened.

---

[*] I discuss interracial contact in later chapters.

The often negative images and stereotypes that lingered, bolstered by residential separation, made it tough for me to feel equal to my white classmates. I had little control over the big picture in America at that time.

The Urban Landscape

Whites were leaving, some would say "fleeing," urban America as more Blacks were moving in. For many the exodus to the suburbs represented a step up to a higher quality of life. For African Americans, the arrival in urban America from rural America, in search of better circumstances at the same time whites were leaving, occurred just when America was losing its once mighty manufacturing base that had been used by many of the parents and grandparents of my classmates to secure an economic foothold in urban America. The continued loss of the manufacturing sector has made it harder for many African American families in urban America to make ends meet, hold families together, send their kids to college and to feel the same rosy optimism about the future that millions of my classmates' grandparents felt based on the stories told by their grandchildren, when they lived in the cities.

When millions of African Americans made the big push to urban American from rural areas, their arrival aroused fear that the quality of life in white neighborhoods would diminish.[10][*] Steinberg wrote in his book, *The Ethnic Myth*, about the fear whites had of African Americans:

> The migration of blacks to northern cities and the rising level of racial protest have exacerbated the historic rivalry between immigrants and blacks. Wherever blacks went, it seemed that one or another ethnic group occupied the stratum just above them, and therefore black efforts for self-advancement tended to arouse ethnic loyalties and provoke an ethnic response....
> ...What is feared is not racial contamination, but reduced property values; not racial mixing, but deteriorating neighborhoods and schools. At bottom, the so-called ethnic backlash is a conflict between the racial have-nots and the ethnics who have a little and are afraid of losing even that.[11]

The departure of white ethnics to the suburbs while middle class jobs were expanding in the suburbs may have produced a greater unity among whites.

---

[*] See Blumer, "Race Prejudice as a Sense of Group Position," 1958. Our fear of losing what we have gained, our sense of relative deprivation to another group when we compare our lifestyle is important to consider. Social psychological research in the 1950's placed emphasis on social comparison theory. Sheriff's work with young boys at a day camp showed how easy it was to create a sense of "our group" against "your group" (Ross and Nisbett, 1991). Festinger's and Stouffer's work examined how individual's came to have a "frame of reference" that was often associated with a particular group at a given time.

White ethnics were not fully accepted as white prior to World War II.[12] Not only was there economic mobility for white ethnics after the war, but the arrival of African Americans into core urban areas, which gave African Americans greater visibility, may have pushed whites to close ranks.[13]

To be white then and now still meant to push away or distance oneself from the "other" race.[*] I often feel that until the two groups share the same resources, live in the same neighborhoods, share similar social networks (important for obtaining resources such as job leads), each "side" will feel different from the other for the foreseeable future. Growing up I had to acknowledge and sometimes outwardly accept the negative images of African Americans some whites harbored. I was very aware of the stigmas associated with being African American.[†]

Fueled by an over exposure by African Americans to a rapidly aging and archaic industrial sector in comparison to the over exposure of whites to the new service-oriented post-industrial America in suburbia, today members of each group still feel a sense of great social distance from each other. Our sense of difference is often attributed to possible cultural differences. On the other hand, our sense of difference could also hinge on the great disparity in living conditions members of each group still encounter.

I was quietly very proud to be African American. In addition to my alternative community created by my parents, frequent trips to Temple University in the 60's and early 70's where my mother was a professor, riding through very poor neighborhoods, certainly gave me a multitude of alternative perspectives to those embraced by classmates and neighbors. My suburban world of tree-lined streets and innocence was challenged on these trips. Graffiti scribbled on the remaining walls of decaying houses on the way to Temple University, once home to white ethnics, one that said "Free Bobby," in reference to Black

---

[*] I discuss in later chapters the current massive movement of whites away from suburbs as African Americans have pushed out from urban America to the inner rings of the suburbs.

[†] My immediate world in the 1960's was based on the elements of the school reader with the central characters of Dick, Jane and Spot. It was a world that reflected the recent massive expansion of the suburbs by urban working class whites, like pioneers in a new land, but aided by low interest housing loans and college tuition plans accessible to millions of white soldiers who had fought in World War II. The same benefits given to white servicemen were intentionally denied by the government to African American servicemen. See Brodkin, "How Jews Became White Folks," 2002. Brodkin argued that the government by not giving out a fair share of low interest housing loans to African Americans in proportion to the number given out to whites, played a big role in producing the residential racial separation found in many suburbs today. But I point out to my students that we are all victims of our very recent past. Our current lack of contact, residential segregation and feelings of cultural difference are a result of the actions of our parents' and grandparents' generations.

Panther, Bobby Seal, certainly opened my eyes to the existence of another world and another perspective. To see and be with African Americans confirmed that there were alternative standards of beauty, culture and vantage points, alternates to those advanced by a "white" media" that were often readily endorsed by my classmates.[*]

Apprehension

I was quite concerned about attending Upper Darby High School and being one of two or three African Americans in a school of nearly 2000 whites.[†] Although my sister would elect to attend, I instead went to a small, private, Quaker Friends' school. In contrast to the nearly 700 students who would have been in my graduating class, there were only 57 at my private high school.

Both my parents worked. In fact most of the West Philadelphian club families were middle class and dual-income families – a precursor for what was to come for middle class white families later in the mid to late 70's to the present when it would become much more difficult to support a family with one income.

West Philadelphian married couples were quite traditional, working class values, even though both partners usually worked outside the home and together would be considered middle to upper-middle class. My parents' combined income was probably greater than most of my classmates' parents in elementary or junior high school not only because both of my parents worked, but both of my parents were college educated. My mom earned a doctoral degree when I was in middle school. An undergraduate degree, when I was growing up, was still rather unique, regardless of the race of the recipient. Parents who wanted their kids to go to college made sure their children took classes while in high school that prepared them for higher education rather than a curriculum that was considered vocationally oriented.

Out of all of the 70 or so classmates from my final year in elementary school, 6th grade, although many went to college, I was the only one to obtain a doctorate. I don't think they felt the same urgency that I did to attend graduate

---

[*] It was reported in a New York Times' article that in Manhattan the top fifth of earners make 52 times more than the bottom fifth or 98 cents on every dollar. Roberts, "In Manhattan", 2005. Such disparities between the top income earners and those on the bottom, who are disproportionately African American, serve to maintain feelings of "racial difference." Such disparities also serve to limit prolonged positive contact given that the two groups often do not reside in the same neighborhoods. Social spaces shared by members of each group, residentially and occupationally, may enable Americans to reduce, limit or even eliminate the use of the term race as a primary descriptor.

[†] Moyer's research indicated that in 1960, 42.6% of the males in Upper Darby did manual labor and in 1970 the figure rose to 45.6%. The women in Upper Darby in 1960 and 1970 respectively engaged in non-manual labor, 76.2% and 79.8%. Women were heavily employed in clerical work. Moyer, *Sociopolitical Attitudes*, 1980.

school.* Unlike many of my classmates, I knew from a very early age that I would go to college. For some of my classmates there seemed to be alternative paths to happiness or life satisfaction while making a living, rather than attending college and certainly instead of going on and getting a doctorate.

Socially it was easier for them. Thus, in planning a future, I don't think the absence of graduate school credentials was seen as limiting or preventing one from having the "good life." Whereas I felt it was important, still do, to have a graduate degree in order to have more life choices in terms of where to live and whom I have contact with now and in the future.

My High School Years

At my private high school, there was a critical mass of African Americans for the first time in a school that I attended. There were only about 10 to 15 spread out over three grades, but this was a sizeable number to me, all of whom I knew quite well given the small size of the school. Their parents represented a variety of occupational backgrounds. There was probably an over representation who were doctors. There were some who owned small businesses. Although affluent, very few lived in the suburbs. Most lived in Mount Airy or Germantown, areas still within Philadelphia, or in West Philadelphia.

I regularly traveled with other African American students on weekends to parties not only in the suburbs but to many neighborhoods in Philadelphia including the poorer areas of the city. The parties in Philadelphia were held in the basements of African American households. Perhaps the city was safer then. We rarely knew who owned the house or the parents of the teenager who gave the party. I do not recall ever seeing alcohol or even smelling alcohol on the breath of someone at those parties. The parties were packed wall to wall. One had to literally push through the crowds. Violence was rare at these parties.

There was some marijuana. It was never smoked in the house. I don't recall the use of other drugs. The parties were all about dancing, 3 or 4 fast songs and then a slow song or two to literally do a "grind," pressing one's hips against those of someone else you almost never knew but just happened to ask to dance because she was standing against the wall or talking to her friend. Although seemingly risqué, it was all very innocent play. This was in the early to mid 70's, the pre-disco era, when dances like the "bump" were fashionable. The

---

* As strange as it may seem, I actually attended my sixth grade reunion about five years ago. Nearly three quarters of the students showed. For me it was quite meaningful. I didn't attend high school with them so I didn't know how they had spent those years. In a sense I wanted to know what they had done during that time and what I had missed. But something had brought them to the reunion as well. Perhaps 6th grade represented the loss of innocence - the following year we all went to middle school. Perhaps 6th grade was meaningful because the year was 1968. King and Robert Kennedy were assassinated then.

parties were never racially mixed. There was never a moment at a party where people stood without music and talked. The core of each party was dancing and the lights were kept very low.

We also went to parties at other private schools, most were located deep in the suburbs; some were at private boarding schools. Each of these schools had a small number of African Americans at this time, not many, but enough, similar to my high school, to form a Black Student Union and thereby capable of organizing social functions. Regardless of where the party was, in a basement in a very poor section of Philadelphia, or at an elite boarding school on Philadelphia's Main Line, the same culture existed, dancing and more dancing.

Parties thrown by our white classmates were attended as well. It wasn't a two-way street. They never came to "ours," those that we would drop in on in the city, or even those we had at our own houses, but we always were invited and went to "theirs." Parties thrown by white classmates tended to be more spontaneous, parents were often not at home and alcohol was much more prevalent. This was in complete contrast to the African American parties. There was never dancing. The lights were always on. The people who attended were usually known by someone, whereas the parties we attended in Philadelphia seemed to be open to the public.[*]

Black and White Cultural Differences

One can easily believe that African Americans and whites have very different cultures. But, one can also conclude that differences in cultural practice can be attributed to class differences between the two races, given that African Americans and whites had and continue to have access to different resources – thus each group has been continually exposed throughout history to a different set of life experiences. One can argue that cultural differences that existed between the black and white parties I attended while in high school, differences that still exist on college campuses today, may actually be related to different types of resources found in more urban versus suburban areas. The overwhelming majority of whites who attended my high school were from the suburbs. The characteristics of the parties I attended in numerous sections of Philadelphia were probably similar to the parties that the parents of my classmates in elementary school would have attended when they lived in urban America before moving to the suburbs. The parties would have been in the basement of houses, more open to the public, and with more dancing.

Although my social life changed significantly in high school, the many friends I had in my neighborhood, elementary and junior high school continue to have a profound influence on my life today. They, especially those who lived

---

[*] One can conclude based on work by William Julius Wilson and Elijah Anderson that indeed urban places may have been safer in the early 70's compared to today.

nearby, made me who I am today, just as much as my feelings of being black, societal images and stereotypes that I still encounter on a daily bases, continue to influence my identity. Although my white classmates pushed me to feel like I was the norm, their norm, I also knew that I was not like them, that I was different. I did not have the same range of social experiences that they had, the same free access to all the places that they did.[*]

Perceptions and feelings of difference

Although I do not recall the particular college class, I remember a professor who pointed out that a possible explanation for the burning of witches in the Salem area during the Colonial time period was that those who were burned lived in areas that were different from those who cast the accusations and that those who were persecuted dressed differently, especially the women who wore strange hats that could not be explained from a distance. Although we live in a society today that some sociologists now describe as color blind, referring to what many Americans want to believe as opposed to what they really feel and practice with each other, there is still often a deep sense of estrangement between African Americans and whites.[†] Some of us more than others are able to operate more smoothly on both sides of the fence. One possible reason for the feelings of difference between African Americans and whites is that whites tend to be over represented in suburban and rural areas and African Americans are still in urban areas or areas immediately adjacent to cities and thus life experiences vary based on the characteristics of living in different geographic locations – different social networks and job opportunities.

Strangely, in terms of social distance, there is often a sense of divide, a caste system in America that harkens back through many generations. Although one could argue that this sense of estrangement is related to different cultural practices, it is just as easy to consider that the origins of a modern-day estrangement are based on the fact that so many African Americans are experiencing and can expect a different quality of life than whites, even when African American and white families have comparable resources and achievements.[‡]

I experienced similar feelings of difference when I was younger. In junior high school, in the late 60's to the early 70's, I remember being in the locker room after gym class and a classmate wanted to know why there had been a fight between African Americans in West Philadelphia and whites from the

---

[*] My father must have had similar feelings. He attended Penn State in the 1940's and was not allowed to live in the freshman dormitories because of his race.

[†] See Tyrone A. Forman, "Color-blind Racism and Racial Indifference", 2004.

[‡] See Shapiro's work on different levels of wealth between African Americans and whites, *The Hidden Cost of Being African American*, 2004.

adjacent suburb of Upper Darby where I grew up. The fight had supposedly taken place in a park that straddled the border with Philadelphia. "Why do you people do that?" I was asked.

Now that I recall this incident decades later, and it is pretty vivid because I can still picture the setting and remember who asked me the question, I wonder why it didn't occur to me at that moment, or throughout the immediate years after, that his question was very one sided, our team against their team, in-group versus out-group. He didn't question why whites from Upper Darby would be involved in the fight. Perhaps deep down there was an assumption, perhaps I had internalized it as well, that those who were African American were naturally the bad guys. I do not remember my response but it was probably to indicate that I didn't have a clue. I believe similar messages today emanate from the media when we see countless sound bites of crime in urban America without examination of the root causes of crime and do not hear much discussion of corporate crime by those who reside in the suburbs.

There was great awareness by whites when I was growing up of the recent move to Philadelphia by African Americans particularly to sections of the city that bordered Upper Darby. It was only years later, well after I had graduated from college, that African Americans made inroads into those fringe areas outside of the city near West Philadelphia. The beginning forays were by those African Americans who took up residence in some of the apartment complexes in Upper Darby near West Philadelphia. Visually, the pattern of dispersion seemed to follow a classic urban sociology text, the spreading out from the city along major arteries such as significant highways and railroad lines. Apartment complexes seemed to be a primary means to do so.

At What Price?

By the mid-1960's, West Philadelphia had become solidly African American. There seemed to be an invisible residential wall down the middle of 63rd Street, the road that officially separated city and Upper Darby. On one side lived African Americans and on the other whites. Moyer wrote:

> In 1960, about 0.17% of the total population [Upper Darby] was black and in 1970, this figure was 0.16%. The only census tract in which more than 1% of the population was black in 1970 is made up almost entirely of an apartment complex where blacks rent housing units, but were not buying property to become relatively permanent township residents....The western portion of Philadelphia is predominantly black, with only Cobbs Creek and Cobbs Creek Park serving as territorial boundaries between West Philadelphia and Upper Darby.[*]

---

[*] Moyer, *Sociopolitical Attitudes*, 1980, pg. 7. It may be of interest to note, according to Moyer that although Upper Darby was essentially all white, it was ethnically diverse.

My classmates needed information about African Americans and I was it. Even my middle school social studies teacher one day, with good intentions, said in front of the class, "Bob, if you have thoughts about the upcoming topic [a unit on African Americans was to be taught], please tell us," and I was being raised in the suburbs like they were! It was a nice gesture on his part. But I just wanted to be a kid, probably a "white kid," like the rest of my classmates and I couldn't. I didn't have any substantial knowledge of social events, at least not more than most of my classmates. I was there to learn like everyone else.

There was a teacher who was openly agitated or anxious over my social intimacy with my classmates. I remember talking a little too much in my middle school math class, actually not more than a sentence to a girl next to me, and promptly being asked to sit in the back of the room. Although my classmate had initiated the conversation, she was not asked to move.

My light skin didn't allow me full access to the world my classmates experienced. They didn't mean for me to feel embarrassed but the stigmas against African Americans were so heavy and strong at that time, I couldn't help but shrink and cringe. There was little to any formal or informal contact between African Americans and whites in the suburbs then. There is still minimal contact in many areas. Sometimes they would joke and use the "n" word to describe African Americans and just as fast apologize to me, "we didn't mean you." What a schizophrenic world I lived in. I wasn't that "n" to my friends, yet I certainly was.

Hearing a report on the news of a crime allegedly committed by an African American, I felt the shame of being the representative to supposed knowledge of these acts of deviant behavior. "Why do *YOUR* people do that?" I should have responded emphatically, "*I* didn't do it!" But being the good ambassador, I simply shrugged my shoulders, continued to let the ball lie in their court and waited for more shoes to drop. They had no contact with African Americans. Nor did they have any contact with urban social problems. Their world was very different than the world in the city. Again, one is reminded that although multiculturalism, respect for differences, was being born, this was still a period with a heavy emphasis on assimilation. Minority groups were expected to conform to a lifestyle that the majority of whites were experiencing in suburban America.

More and more African Americans were becoming visible particularly through the media, although still somewhat of a new phenomenon, during the

---

Between 28 and 30% of the population was either foreign-born or reported a foreign-born parent. Over thirteen different major ethnic backgrounds were represented, Moyer wrote. She further indicated that in both the 1960 and 1970 census, over 25% of those of foreign stock were of Italian heritage, almost 20% were of Irish background, and about 16% claimed a connection to the United Kingdom Moyer, *Sociopolitical Attitudes*, pg. 9.

time I was a child. Jackie Robinson had broken the color barrier in "white" professional baseball only eleven years prior to my parents moving to Upper Darby. Kids in my neighborhood didn't like the excitement the "new" African American athletes sometimes displayed, "be humble, stop being so flamboyant," they would tell me, as if I had control over the behavior of others. Jackie Robinson was anything but flamboyant and I was absolutely shy if not introverted.

In the award-winning documentary, *Eyes on the Prize*, narrated by Georgia state senator Julian Bond, about the post World War II civil rights movement, Muhammad Ali is described as a "boastful" athlete in comparison to his opponent, Floyd Patterson, the reigning champion. Bond indicated that America wanted Patterson to defeat Ali because Patterson, African American, was seen as a "humble" fighter, thus not as "uppity."

I had many friends in elementary school yet I knew very well the enormous social difference many felt from African Americans. They could not see or feel, nor could I fully do so, the conditions of inequality African Americans faced at that time and that I saw on trips to North Philadelphia to Temple's main campus.[14] Their parents, as well as mine, had left those areas where African Americans were moving to by the tens of thousands. Their world was invisible to many African Americans and vice versa. A more profound sense of social difference existed for my generation than for my parents' generation.[15]

Many urban Catholic churches shut their doors and opened new ones outside the city, near my parents' house because they had lost the bulk of their parishioners, white ethnics from Southern and Eastern Europe.

> Upper Darby has almost as many Catholic parochial schools as it has public elementary schools, and in 1960, of the children enrolled kindergarten through high school, 48.9% were in public schools and 51.1% were in nonpublic schools.[16]

Perhaps retaining the experiences of their descendants in urban America, the new "white" arrivals in suburbia continued to espouse the Horatio Alger rags to riches characteristics such as pull yourself up by your own bootstraps.[17] For their parents and grandparents, economic ascendancy was certainly an attainable goal.[18] But when they left urban America, the factories their parents and grandparents had used for mobility, began to close their doors and to move to other countries.

It isn't the same living in urban America as it once was.[19] Southern and Eastern Europeans could more easily say or feel, "if you work hard, anyone in America can make it." Perhaps that belief has carried over to many who live in the suburbs today, passed down from one generation to the next. Today's groups in urban America have a much tougher road and cannot easily be as optimistic because literally millions of factory jobs are now overseas where labor is cheaper. Eastern and Southern Europeans were never asked to have a college degree to make ends meet; whereas, many in urban America today are told to do so. There is no alternative.

People in poor areas of urban and rural America, regardless of race, are now required to jump immediately up the class ladder by going to college. Many of these jobs that now require a college degree or even a master's degree existed for our great grandparents and required much less education. The greater call for credentials as the suburbs mushroomed in size and African Americans arrived by the millions in urban America has continued to fuel a sense of difference between members of each race given that those in suburbia attend better quality schools and are more likely than those from urban America to be successful in higher education and thus obtaining those credentials.

Although my classmates were more liberal than their parents on many issues including cohabitation and intimacy, they had no direct experience with people of color, except for me a very fair African American child who spoke "just like they did." In fact when I went off to college in the Midwest, I remember being told I had a white ethnic accent when I spoke compared to the pristine voices of many white Midwesterners.

When my sister began to think about boys in a more serious way, she began to spend more time in North Philadelphia on or near the Temple campus with African American kids her own age. She suddenly had people of the opposite sex calling her for the first time, from North Philadelphia, and "talking to her." I don't recall her ever receiving a phone call from a white boy when she was in middle school. Her self esteem seemed to rise to incredible heights overnight. It was easy to tell the race of the person my sister was talking to on the phone. Her girlfriends were both African American and white. The inflections in her voice would dramatically change.

Black Power and Multiculturalism

Black Power movements and ideas associated with multiculturalism became very meaningful to me about 6th grade because they exposed how different the quality of life was for African Americans compared to whites. These movements and ideas held less value for my classmates and neighbors since they potentially called for change in the status quo. My father, who had more of a working class identity, was reluctant to embrace Black Power and multicultural ideas, perhaps thinking it was a little too "forward" or "in your face." My mother understood it, felt it, embraced it, and identified with many of her students who understood what was at stake. One of the prominent goals, to summarize the movement, was the desire for equality immediately. Whereas, I think for my father, and many other African Americans of his generation, World War II generation, there was a feeling that the quest for equality should go forward but efforts and strides should be calculated for fear of angering whites.

Internal struggles among African Americans existed as well. The group US pushed for cultural awareness. On the other hand the Black Panthers, a Marxist organization, called attention to class inequalities.[20] The Black Panthers of the 1960's ceased to exist; whereas, multiculturalism remains, perhaps seen as a safer alternative by both whites and African Americans.

When I was growing up, animosity toward African Americans was more direct and open and much more interpersonal. Today it is not nearly as common to hear or read about negative verbal exchanges. The remaining racism today for many sociologists is related to the quality of life each group experiences relative to the other. We are often unaware of just how hard life can be for those who do not share similar life circumstances especially given the enormous racial and class residential segregation that still exists in our society.

I am African American now just like I was when growing up. Who I am supposed to be is often still defined by what race others perceive me to be. Group membership, identity and even personal identity are therefore defined by the experiences the group as a whole has in relation to the overall structure of our society compared to another group: the quality of housing and schools, racial and class segregated social networks, exposure to more crime prone areas, poor medical care and more.

When I was a child, I was approached with skepticism by some of my friends' parents. My hair was different to them, soft and "wooly," a word used by some. It wasn't uncommon for my classmates to touch my head to feel my hair. "Why is your hair different?" one parent loved to ask me. This particular parent when he said "your" meant all African Americans and not just me. He was never able to see me as a person. Years later on a summer evening when I was a teenager, he called his daughter inside to prevent us from talking to each other. I never had a significant conversation with her again.

In the neighborhood where I was raised, any attempt to discuss issues related to race was not possible, it meant to complain.[21] To discuss what it meant to be black was to make waves and to be accused of reverse racism. "If you just don't talk about being African American, don't make it an issue, everything will be fine." Or, "if we see you with another African American, you must be plotting something." That was impossible since it would have been hard to find another African American in my public school. Yet African Americans were continually seen as part of a separate and distinct group. Bad behavior by a few African Americans served to indict all.

Conclusion

Today I still feel whiteness on a daily basis. It is "keep your nose clean, be humble, don't make waves and everything will work itself out." To do otherwise is to seek special privilege and call attention to yourself – to be egocentric, self-centered and to have a *black* or radical consciousness. To discuss social problems as they may affect African Americans, for example, the number of children raised in single head-of-household families, is sometimes felt by some white students, not all, and some African American students as well, as too liberal. Social problems today are seen as products of individual accomplishment or failure. We often fail to see, perhaps intentionally, that others suffer from similar problems and thus there may exist patterns of behavior influenced by common negative social forces in our society that affect many people both African American and white and not just the individual.

In terms of my appearance, it was not always easy to "racially" or ethnically *place* me. My fair skin allowed (-s) me to have more access to "whites" when I was growing up than someone who had darker skin than mine. I could entertain dating and marrying whites whereas for my sister, someone who had darker skin, her acceptance seemed to me somewhat more difficult and abrasive to her classmates. Her self-esteem as a "Black" female was challenged in different ways than my masculinity as a "Black" male.[22] Perhaps this is why there are far more African American male/white female couples today than white male/African American female. Hurtado wrote:

> Now, as then, white middle-class women are groomed from birth to be the lovers, mothers, and partners (however unequal) of white men because of the economic and social benefits attached to these roles.[23]

> The definition of woman is constructed differently for white women and for women of Color, though sexuality is the marking mechanism through which the subordination of each is maintained. The construction of white womanhood also eroticizes potency (as male) and victimization/frailty (as female).[24]

We still live in a sexist society and standards of beauty are still more important to women than men in terms of self worth.

Although I am very fair, I would like to think that I have always stood proud and identified as an African American even when the cards were stacked against me and the penalty could have been great for openly admitting who I was. However, I do remember when I was in elementary and junior high school quite vividly instances, usually when there was a crowd of people and the discussion was about race and I was the lone African American, when I did remain silent and kept my mouth shut with a severe case of internal cognitive dissonance.

I show my students a few minutes of the film, *Imitation of Life*, made about 60 years ago. The light-skin daughter passes as white and denies knowing her darker mother when the mother comes to visit the daughter while at the daughter's place of employment. A lot was at stake then. For the daughter it meant whether she would keep her job or not. Exposure as African American would have meant the loss of her job and thus a different lifestyle for her.

A close relative told me that a great uncle, who was white, did cut off contact with the family because he didn't want to be associated with African Americans. In a society that preaches individualism, the continued existence of racial categories is an inherent contradiction.

Chapter Two
Invisibility

As a child, I didn't dare go to one of the swim clubs to which my white classmates had access. I would not have been accepted by those who did not know me. So my parents took my sister and me to the swim club in Yeadon.[25] The African American families in Yeadon, because they could not use a nearby swimming pool used by whites, built their own club and called it the *Nile*. There was little diversity at our club. There was one interracial couple. He was African American and she was white.

On one of my recent trips back to my parents' house, I took my children to a playground next to the *Nile*. There were five or so African American children there. I sat on a bench watching my three children play. They had only been exposed to areas that were overwhelmingly white and rural. My soon-to-be first grader came over to me, sat down and quietly asked, "Dad, why are we the only white people here?" I leaned over and whispered in his ear, whispering to make the moment more dramatic, "because we aren't white." For a moment he was like a deer caught in the headlights of a car. But he understood.

The following semester my family accompanied me on sabbatical. We lived on campus at the University of Waterloo, Ontario, in graduate and family housing. My children not only played with kids from countries all over the world but attended the most diverse public school in the region. It was a breath of needed fresh air.

I have considered living in Canada, since it is so close, to escape feelings of racial type-casting and the sense of difference I frequently feel at home in the

States. I would be able to visit my parents more easily if I were to live north of the border than if I were to live overseas. My somewhat frequent visits to Canada, and subsequent conversations with Canadian students, both undergraduate and graduate, faculty and ordinary citizens have convinced me that although life could be better in Canada, there is also racism there, though much more subtle. My constant state of transience has prevented me from fully feeling the possibility that Canadians also have biases and prejudicial feelings toward non-white Canadians.

It is possible that Canadians are quite different, or can temporarily cast aside commitment to a serious dialogue on racism given that African Canadians are only 2% of a total population of close to thirty million people. Perhaps many Canadians simply do not feel threatened by African Canadians, or feel the same need as some in the States to confront issues related to race.*†

Although I have thought about living in Canada, I also think about what it would mean to have a sense of belonging. Meaning, although I often do not feel like the norm in America, someone who can walk and be seen by others without being *raced*, I feel I have a very strong case that I am *American*, perhaps, boastful-like, more American than others because I am African American. My American-ness is extremely strong whereas my Canadian-ness would be new to me, and to other Canadians, thus weaker.

A strong case can be made that African Americans played a huge part in building and making America great, enabling others to collect and organize capital that was used for the foundation for an industrial era and now a post industrial era.[26] The labor and toil of African Americans aided and allowed the construction of future infrastructures that were the bedrock and means for immigrants to come to America. African Americans fought in every

---

* Other issues may take center stage such as the separatist movement in Quebec and rights for First Nation groups.
† It is intriguing to note that I have never taught a class where prior to the start of the class the majority of students knew the actual percentage of African Americans in the United States. Students tend to inflate the actual percentage by about two and a half times from roughly 12% to about thirty. Odd, but this was also the case with my Canadian students in the class I taught while on sabbatical at the University of Waterloo. Apparently knowledge about issues related to race and stereotypes held by many Americans about other Americans is also known and accepted by many Canadians about Americans.

Table 1. Total Canadian and Visible Minority Population Groups

Total population	29,639,035 (100%)
Total visible minority population	3,983,845 (13%)
Black	662,210 (2%)
South Asian	917,075 (3%)
Chinese	1,029,395 (3.5%)
Korean	100,660 (<1%)
Japanese	73,315 (<1%)
Southeast Asian	198,880 (<1%)
Filipino	308,575 (1%)
Arab/West Asian	303,965 (1%)
Latin American	216,975 (<1%)
Visible minority, not included elsewhere	98,920 (<1%)
Multiple visible minority	73,875 (<1%)

Extracted from *Visible minority population, by provinces and territories (2001 Census)* table, Stats Canada.

war for their (our) freedom and that perhaps if they had not fought in the Revolutionary War America might not have gained its independence from Britain.[27] I can prove and feel my American-ness very strongly, wear it with pride, with a genuine air in ways that perhaps many European Americans (whites) are unable.

The dialogue within the Canadian "mosaic" is still not as fully developed for African Canadians as it is in the United States for African Americans. There seems to be a stronger invisibility there. But that isn't to say that the ground would not be fertile in Canada; that with time, I *could* feel the same pride, the same linkages and the same level of Canadian-ness as I feel my American-ness. There was slavery in Canada, although it ended about 30 years earlier. There was segregation especially in Quebec Province on public transportation in Montreal well into the 1960s. Possibly thousands of slaves, certainly hundreds, ran away to Canada to escape slavery in the United States. African American loyalists escaped to Nova Scotia after the American Revolution.

Thus I could claim a direct connection to the roots of Canadian history if I lived in Canada and were to identify as an African Canadian, or just Canadian. But that dialogue in Canada is still to be unearthed. It is dormant, fallow with little tillage. Perhaps ignorance would be more bliss and to remain unearthed would allow greater invisibility for me. Perhaps I would experience a greater sense of self, something I often feel I want more of in America. Perhaps I would be able to escape the stereotypes or characteristics that mark African Americans.

The Introduction of Race

"Race" as a marker and its use as a method of systematically controlling perceived groups of people are relatively new to humankind. Even in North America, its introduction was not automatic. Bennett wrote that there was a period of time before the United States was founded when Africans and Europeans in America did not recognize racial distinctions.

> Working together in the same fields, sharing the same huts, the same situation, and the same grievances, the first black and white Americans, aristocrats excepted, developed strong bonds of sympathy and mutuality. They ran away together, played together and revolted together. They mated and married, siring a sizeable mixed population. In the process the black and white servants – the majority of the colonial population – created a racial wonderland that seems somehow un-American in its lack of obsession about race and color...
> Of all the improbable aspects of this situation, the oddest – to modern blacks and whites – is that white people did not seem to know that they were white. It appears from surviving evidence that the first white colonists had no concept of themselves as *white* people....The word white...developed late in the century as a direct development of slavery and the organized debasement of blacks...The same point can be made from the other side of the line [Africans did not know they were black]. [28]

I have traced my ancestors back to the time of the Revolutionary War on my father's side. My mother's side goes to the Caribbean to a lineage that has had more recent race mixing.[*] My maternal grandmother was Scottish and her mother was Irish. My father's side is more unknown to me. I crave to know how my skin, his skin, became so light. Who were my ancestors on my father's side? I spent a couple years of serious endeavor finding "his people." It is a classic story of investigation and intrigue, e.g., meandering down narrow windowless hallways at the National Archives in Washington D.C., climbing over misplaced boxes on shelves and eventually locating one hundred pages of Revolutionary War pension records all pertaining to one person directly related to me. It is an investigation that produced many hopeful leads that often led me astray, raised hopes and pushed me to conclude that I may not be able to find all the pieces. Even though on my father's side I have documented a history of very fair complexions stretching back to the Revolutionary War, fairer complexions than many of the immigrants who came to America from Southern and Eastern

---

[*] I never heard my maternal grandmother discuss race or indicate how she identified herself. She was white but this was never discussed

Europe, I have yet to find a white person in my ancestry on his side. I am a descendent of Free Negroes stretching back at least to the Revolutionary War.

My great-great grandfather, Morris Moore, was one of only a handful of African Americans who owned land in Northumberland County, Virginia, prior to the Civil War. He, along with Emily Howland, a wealthy Quaker woman from upstate New York, founded a school for black and white children in Heathesville, the county seat. The school still stands and is now a state and federal landmark. Morris Moore's second marriage was to Margaret Laws my great-great grandmother. The Laws were also Free Negroes. It is from her family that I can trace my roots directly back to three African American men who fought in the Virginia navy during the Revolutionary War on ships such as the Tempest, Defiance and the Mosquito.

One of my ancestors, Timothy Laws, one of three brothers who fought in the Revolutionary War, was nicknamed Brown Sugar, according to pension records filed by his descendents who sought land owed to him for his service. Although they were "free," they had to register every three years in the Registry of Free Negroes. Every county in Virginia had a registry. It recorded skin color, height, and any physical abnormalities such as scars. Thus it is possible to know the skin color of my ancestors on my father's side stretching back to the very early 1800s.

> In 1793, the Virginia General Assembly passed a law requiring all free blacks and mulattoes to go to the courthouse to have their presence in the county registered, and to be given a number. All registrations were recorded in books in the court clerk's office. Such registration would include name, age, color, and also the reason for, or condition of freedom. Each year, every registrant was to return to the courthouse to purchase a copy at a cost of 25 (cents). Once every three years each registrant was to obtain a new certificate. This certificate was to be kept on the person's body at all times when away from home. Failure to produce the certificate on demand from a white person was sufficient cause to be sold into slavery for failure to prove one's status as a free person of color. [29]

The following individual is listed in the *Northumberland County, Virginia Register of Free Negroes, 1803-1849,* and is an example of a typical entry in the registry.[30] Daniel Laws was my great-great-great grandfather.

[1844]

Daniel Laws bright   46   5'6"h   a scar on the right eyebrow
         Born free   June 10th

Over 600 entries were made in the registry for Northumberland County. In the case of Daniel Laws, above, "bright" refers to the color of his skin and often signified someone who was quite fair. His height was 5'6." The registry also indicated that he had a scar, that he was born free and that he was registered on June 10, 1844 (indicated earlier on the same page of the Registry).

Historically, in only two locations in America (New Orleans and Charleston) was there ever serious consideration of racial categories other than black and white. In fact, as time passes after the Civil War, the more stringent the definition of who was white became, influenced by scientific racism and the eugenics movement. In the early part of the 20th century Virginia passed laws that defined even those with a little African American ancestry as African American.

> ...The fourteen remaining Southern states considered a definition essential, and seven of them adopted the one-drop rule by defining a Negro as someone with any black ancestry. Virginia finally abandoned its one-fourth rule in 1910 and settled for one-sixteenth, assuming that lesser amounts could not be detected. Not until 1930 did Virginia adopt the one-drop rule explicitly, saying that "any Negro blood at all" makes a person black. [31]

> Lawsuits testing the legality of the one-drop rule have been infrequent ever since the federal courts so unequivocally endorsed the well-known custom of defining anyone with even a single black ancestor as a black person. The Phipps case (Jane Doe v. State of Louisiana) was big news nationally in 1983, largely because of its rarity. When the state presented genealogical evidence that allegedly showed Mrs. Phipps and her siblings to be three thirty-seconds black, the courts of Louisiana at all three levels, and the U.S. Supreme Court, left the "traceable amount rule" (the one-drop rule) undisturbed. [32]

My father's mother was Native American. According to oral history from my relatives, there were other Native Americans as well, in the early 1800s directly related. These stories include physical features such as having long straight black hair as well as a fair shade of skin. Some probably could have passed for white, although I know of no one on my father's side who did. My father's uncle reportedly had blue eyes, white skin and wavy hair. He did not try to pass. We were and still do think of ourselves as people of color, specifically African American.

My father, with his wavy hair and almost white skin, could have "gotten away with it" should he have chosen to do so. My mother with her somewhat straight hair might have pulled it off too but she would have been "stuck" when confronted about her somewhat darker skin. They never contemplated "passing." They couldn't have claimed to be biracial even if they had wanted, because it was not an option at that time. Historically one could not be just a little African American. One was either African American or one was not. Having even a small number of African American ancestors legally in some states meant that you were African American, thus unable to have the same privileges as those who were white. These privileges often included the opportunity to have a good job. Passing for white would have meant separation both psychologically and physically from their families as well.[*]

My father's family arrived in urban America near the start of the 20th century well before the big push by millions of African Americans after World War II. Some of my paternal great-grandfather's siblings went to Baltimore in the late 1800s. They came from rural America, from Northumberland County, Virginia. Baltimore was a logical place to move to given that there were ferries from Lancaster County, adjacent to Northumberland, to Baltimore where there were better economic opportunities. My paternal grandfather went to Philadelphia in the early 1900s and owned a moving company. Because of gas rationing during World War II, he could no longer keep his business going and had to seek other work. He found a job in the shipyard but because of his race he was given a hazardous position and he developed problems with his lungs and died. I never met him. He died well before I was born when my father was in college at Penn State.

Like the other members of the "West Philadelphians," my father was a victim of intense discrimination. Yet he was also in the position to be able to fight for entry into the suburbs in the 1950s. My father and his boyhood friends helped each other out in times of crisis. They gave each other job leads and were able to secure in numerous instances good jobs for their children. They, like their wives, worked hard. Both my parents worked. In fact most of the "West Philadelphian" families were dual-income, middle class families. West Philadelphian married couples were quite traditional, often with working class traditional values, even though both partners worked outside the home. Most were solidly middle class families by the late 60s and mid 70s. Their children became part of the first large wave of African Americans to attend college during the modern Civil Rights era.

The World War II generation fought to break down the initial barriers and to get one's foot in the door. There may have been fear among some that pushing too hard could cause a backlash from white America.[33] For my generation, perhaps sensing we did have more opportunity available to us than our parents, we often pushed the idea that racial separation had its place and it was even necessary in some form so that we could more clearly define what needed to be done to help African Americans. It didn't seem realistic to give power to whites in decision making processes. Thus good planning meant giving power to those most affected by policies and laws.

---

[*] See Haizlip's *The Sweeter the Juice*, 1995, for a genealogical discussion of her family and the many different shades of being African American as well as the historical hardships individuals in her family faced trying to make a living.
[*] Gates, *Colored People*, 1995.

There are parallels here with various feminist movements that developed in the 1960s. My generation broke with earlier traditions of mixed race protests for racial justice.[*] Black Power dictated that African Americans needed to have control of their own destiny and only African Americans knew what was best for African Americans just as only women new what was best for women.

Many whites may have opted out of the struggle today because they believe that equality of opportunity has been achieved and with time a new society will develop and is close at hand. Some may have opted out given that competition in the workforce is felt to be tougher today than in the past and thus affirmative action policies may actually be felt as an immediate threat to job security. Others may no longer feel it was *their place* to be actively involved in the struggle for equality.

Like many whites, some African Americans in my father's generation may have felt a sense of bewilderment, "Why couldn't 'they,' African Americans who were just arriving in urban America, adjust, be more law abiding, speak better English, conform?" But regardless of this internal pecking order among African Americans, sometimes epitomized or stereotyped as light against dark, that historically echoed internal class divisions among African Americans, we were all the same "race." Until the early 1960s we were called *Colored*. In the late 1960s throughout the 1970s, we were Blacks or Afro Americans. In the early 1980's we became African Americans. Although there were internal divisions, e.g., if you were darker than a paper bag, "the paper bag test," you couldn't get into some social functions, we (nor my father's generation) ever heard of something called biracial, even though many of "us" were "more white" than most who claim to be biracial today. Although to be white meant access to a better life and to more resources, my father and I couldn't and wouldn't go that direction. It would have been a sense of shame, an admission that "white America" had made life so psychologically unforgiving that we had eventually caved in and admitted defeat.

The Divide between the races

Other African Americans could have followed my father and mother to the suburbs after World War II if the federal government had not actively denied benefits to African American soldiers. According to Brodkin, the growth of the suburbs was fostered because the government made available millions of low interest housing loans to working class white veterans, who then were able to

---

[*] I went to college in the mid-70s, whereas the Black Power movement on college campuses occurred in the late 60s. I still consider myself to be on the tail end of that time period.

leave urban areas and buy a house outside the city, most in the now older suburban areas that now ring urban America.

> The GI Bill of Rights, as the 1944 Serviceman's Readjustment Act was known, was arguably the most massive affirmative action program in U.S. history. ...
> ....The eleven million military personnel who were demobilized in the 1940s represented a quarter of the U.S. labor force.
> ...The almost eight million GIs who took advantage of their educational benefits...White male GIs were able to take advantage of their educational benefits for college and technical training, so they were particularly well positioned to seize the opportunities provided by the new demands for professional, managerial and technical labor...
> Rather, the military, the Veterans' Administration, the U.S Employment Service, and the Federal Housing Administration (FHA) effectively denied African-American GIs access to their benefits and to the new educational, occupational, and residential opportunities.[34]

As Brodkin argues, the government by not giving out a fair share of low interest housing loans to African Americans in proportion to the number given out to whites, played a big role in producing the residential racial separation that existed in the suburbs when I was growing up. Many of my students believe they are in no way prejudicial or racist. I point out we are all victims of our very recent past. Our current lack of contact, residential segregation and feelings of cultural difference have been heavily influenced by the actions of our parents' and grandparents' generations. If there had not been massive discrimination against African Americans, it is fair to believe that many more African Americans would be living in more integrated suburbs today.[35]

In addition, access to small towns in America was also blocked to African Americans.

> A sundown town is any organized jurisdiction that for decades kept African Americans or other groups from living in it and was thus "all-white" on purpose...
> Outside the traditional South – states historically dominated by slavery, where sundown towns are rare – *probably a majority of all incorporated places kept out African Americans.*[36]

More integrated neighborhoods would exist today, economic integration of African Americans would be stronger, and feelings of difference between the two groups, African American and white, would probably be substantially less.

...Whiteness is meaningless in the absence of Blackness; the same holds in reverse. Moreover, race itself would be meaningless if it were not a fault line along which power, prestige, and respect are distributed. [37]

Our discussion of race today therefore might be quite different had there been less discrimination of African Americans in the very recent past.[38]

II

A Sense of Difference

Chapter Three
Feelings of Discomfort

I have found that students, both African American and white, are very quick to point out that to desire to date someone of one's own race is fine because it is based on "individual preference." I cannot help but feel that there is an inherent contradiction here. On the one hand students in the same breath proclaim that no two people are the same. "Some people like strawberry and others like lime." If we believe so strongly that people are unique, and thus no two people are the same, why do we continue to lump people together into groups called race? Is racial division, particularly black and white, so engrained in the American psyche that we will never be able to get past it and that the best we can hope for is to work around it? Within the range of supposed physical differences between the races there is also great overlap. I have known African Americans to have blond hair and blue eyes. Culturally, who would dare to say that every African American or that every person who identifies as white has a similar culture? Judging from what I hear emanating from dorm windows and sound systems in cars driven by students, rap is listened to by all people regardless of race. Yet racial categories remain.

I find older students do not push the "we are all different" line as often. They do not seem to come with the same rough edges of a heightened individualism that many of my traditional-age college students have fresh out of high school. Age seems to temper the older college student, the cuts and bruises of the real world lessen their ability to be so myopic and inherently contradictory. Perhaps older students are an altogether different clientele who seek a more personal understanding of the world around them and thus when they return to school are more open to a greater variety of ideas and vantage points. They may be less likely to box people into categories.

This past summer one of my traditional-age college students wore a hat with a confederate flag in the upper right hand corner. Feelings of discomfort churned within me. I thought about his right to wear what he wanted. This particular symbol served as a trigger point leading me to feel a greater sense of social distance from this student than usually felt between teacher and student. I was initially reluctant to directly challenge him about his attire, since how one dresses or looks should not be considered relevant by a teacher. Given that the course was about contemporary race relations, it wasn't difficult to weave his hat into the lecture.

The student made an individual choice to dress the way he did, thereby separating his desires from any reaction it may evoke in others. But yet again, the flag only has meaning within the context of lumping individuals together, "it is about culture and pride and not hate" those who wear the flag often state. I cannot help but believe that if the student had significant contact with African Americans on a routine basis he would feel differently about wearing a hat with a confederate flag. He would be aware of the meaning the flag has for so many African Americans.

I, like Congressman John Lewis, am an integrationist.[*] The history of the South should be seen and studied as a unified whole and not separated into parts as if one part, i.e., the experiences of one "race," did not affect and determine the experiences of another "race." Although there is still immense segregation between African Americans and whites, I believe that the two groups are so intricately interwoven, historically, culturally, socially, economically and politically that to try and separate them, to understand one without the other is in vain. Sociologist Larry Griffin wrote:

> ...What I read from an anonymous student about my first "Sociology of the South" course, however shocked me. It read, verbatim: "Blacks, slavery and CR [civil rights] are important but not total. What about our culture?" Because every student in that inaugural "South" offering was white and most from the South, the word "our" in the student's course evaluation

---

[*] For a good narrative and description of the early years of the Civil Rights movement see the book by Lewis and D'Orso, *Walking with the Wind*, 1998, a book about the life of Congressman John Lewis, who was arrested over 40 times for attempting to integrate various facilities and places in the South. The book gives an excellent description and analyses of the tension over whether or not whites should be actively involved in the fight for equality for African Americans in these organizations and the subsequent decrease in their direct involvement.

could have had only one meaning. Simply put, a student had left my class on the South believing, despite what were then my best efforts, in the reality of segregated black and white histories that most certainly did not converge in the American South, believing in the existence of a white regional culture having nothing to do with – and therefore innocent of – African Americans, or slavery, or the black freedom struggle

...My failure to absorb and digest that elemental truth that black southerners were *southerners* and, consequently, that "the South" belonged as much to them as to whites was a failure of vision and empathy, an act of moral blindness more troubling still because my student critic's easy, seemingly natural use of the phrase "our culture" implicated me as a member of his or her whites-only southern culture...

...by defining and framing the South largely, if unknowingly, in terms of *whiteness*, this and similar interpretations make – conceptually, semantically, morally – racially plural southern *cultures* unimaginable, make a bi-racial South impossible, make a syncretic southern culture arising from black and white together inconceivable.[39]

If we are going to have a flag that represents Southern people, we need to find one that is acceptable to all citizens of the South, both black and white.

In some cases students feel it is very natural to live separate lives from members of the other race. Growing up in segregated environments often deprives one of a certain sensitivity of what it means to walk in the shoes of another. After one class a student, white female, told me how she and her family enjoyed reenacting the Civil War time period, dressing up to play various parts. She said it so smoothly, and expressed a desire that should I have the opportunity to partake in such an activity, I should do so without hesitation. I asked her, as we exited the classroom, "what side should I play?" I continued, "I don't think I can play the Civil War game. Do you understand why? I am African American. I can't automatically switch sides or change roles like you can, to reenact the nuances of war on either side. Would I really root for the confederacy to pull out a victory?" She was somewhat stunned. I momentarily witnessed another "deer in the headlights" reaction. It had never occurred to her that I could have difficulty enjoying what she enjoyed so much with her family because of race.

Playing Civil War games was a regular occurrence with some of my friends when I was growing up. I never played, just watched. It just didn't seem right that I should take part in the game. My friends were very knowledgeable and played with such a vivre that they didn't care which side won. I didn't have that luxury even though the war was one hundred years past. African American students sometimes feel a deep sense of social distance from white students.

Although teaching gives me great joy, I sometimes feel devalued as a human being because I teach about issues related to race and thus am reminded routinely about the differences that are felt between people in our country today. If I identified as a member of the majority, I don't think I would be as affected. As a minority, I feel forced to continually evaluate who I am. It feels important to my survival.

Who do I disclose these feelings of discomfort I experience in my classroom when racial differences are exposed? It is absolutely necessary that I have someone to talk to after teaching sometimes five days a week about "race." Listening to students express their biases often makes me wonder what they *really* think of me, similar to some of my white classmates when I was young who talked disparagingly of African Americans not realizing at first I was there. It is quite possible that my fair features allow me to play a more middle of the road role in the classroom, a sort of moderator between two sides. I have known of other situations that involved African American teachers with darker complexions who said the same points that I make in my classroom but who have also caused students to feel divided or even racially pitted against each other. Perhaps my light complexion may enable students, both African American and white, to feel I represent both racial groups. I have been told by students at the end of a course on race that they liked my class because "you didn't take a side." I don't recall one African American ever making a similar comment.

I want to push my students' buttons. I admit that I sometimes aim my lectures at white students more than minorities because I feel that whites as a group have had less exposure to some of the issues discussed in class. Perhaps this is unfair to African American students. It seems that it is white students, though not all, who need to see more or entertain walking in the shoes of another more so than minority groups given that many African Americans on college campuses have had exposure to ideas I express in some of my classes.

"Why are African Americans so many shades?" I ask. I don't think a teacher has ever asked that question to 99% of the white students I have had in my classroom. Nor do I think 99% of white students have ever discussed this topic with a friend. A heightened sense of individualism, "life is what you make it," many believe. Some have been raised to get what they want in life. Their worlds are consensual, viewed with choices and paths taken, prices to pay if one goes the wrong direction. Life is not forced it is voluntary.

For many African American students, part of growing up is to know or have a sense about how the past has influenced the present. African American students may not have all the facts and are indeed wrong or many issues, similar to white students, but there is a sensitivity about issues related to race that exists more so than for many white students and often cuts across economic class lines.

I have found that very few white students have entertained the idea that a significant portion of the differences among skin shades among African

Americans may be the result of non-consensual sex during slavery.* Some have even said the differences in skin shade are because of marriage, forgetting or not knowing that it was against the law in many states up until quite recently for African Americans and whites to marry. In short, one could argue there is little consensual behavior, or less than originally surmised, in the past to explain the wide array of skin shades among African Americans today. African American students seem to "know" this material.

"Why do people live in ghettos?" Very few of my students, white or African American, have an answer to this question. Many believe it is a choice that someone has made. Another answer they may have heard or espouse is that people want to live there. The naiveté of my students hurts me but it can lead to breathtaking feelings of reward and satisfaction as well. I get a lot of pleasure hearing from students, "I never thought of it that way, thanks."

I try and create safe situations where students can meaningfully participate. I have felt from the beginning of my teaching career that teaching must be made personal. My students need to be able to personally connect to ideas found in texts or presented in the classroom. I don't want to brainwash them, just to be able to touch often emotion-laden ideas that already exist in their head, to dispute them, to have those ideas tossed back in my direction to be tackled by me or others in the classroom. I want to learn from my students or else I receive little pleasure as a teacher. If I can create some degree of cognitive dissonance within a student, perhaps all learning is a form of cognitive dissonance, then fine. I want them to think not to memorize.

Each student brings to the table a set of life experiences. A teacher's job is not only to teach what is considered factual information, but to teach lifelong learning skills. Ten years after graduation the facts will change. But if you can teach students how to look at ideas from a multitude of paradigms (including paradigms that the teacher may not personally agree) then you have accomplished something special. The student will continue to think and learn long after they have graduated because they can entertain new facts and ideas and graft them onto paradigms that were learned in the classroom, and even create new paradigms.

Very few of my students want to be seen as prejudicial or, even worse, a racist. For a teacher to raise the possibility that one's personal actions or views

---

* Joel Williamson, *New People: Miscegnation and Mulattoes,* 1995 describes a period in the late 19th and early 20th century as the "Browning of America," a period when African Americans who were "light" married African Americans who were darker, producing an even greater panoply of colors among African Americans. Years ago I asked students to write a short paper on what they believed to be the meaning of the title, *Colored People,* by Henry Louis Gates, Jr. A student turned in a paper with a font that was in as many shades of brown as possible.

could be seen or felt by some as discriminatory can be quite unsettling today. Students, especially from the middle class, are raised to place emphasis on the individual. An emphasis on the individual is often felt to shield one against being accused of bias since patterns of group behavior, being aware that others may feel the same as you, become more obscure.

I believe racism is much more subtle on college campuses today but just as virulent as a generation ago, and with serious consequences.[40] Whom we associate with is important. I believe that if we refuse to cross the line in our social relationships, there is a good chance that we may be reluctant to cross the color line in our professional relationships after graduation. We often choose to work and hire people with whom we associate and we often associate more with people defined as racially similar to us more so than different. We learn feelings of difference at a very early age and often as teenagers and adults attribute socially segregated situations to cultural difference instead of entertaining the idea that race is often defined based on the power and resources of a group more so than supposed cultural differences. Even expected physical differences between two groups defined as being two different races may not be as pronounced as we may think.

Whom We Want to Date and Marry

For me, the "Georgia Peach" and "Southern Belle" conjure up images of white females more so than African American women. The standards of beauty in our society, according to many of my students, are believed to be based on physical appearances more associated with white females. Some African American women are portrayed in the media as quite beautiful, but students may feel that these few individuals do not accurately represent the majority of African American women. Their features may include standards of beauty more associated with white females such as straight hair and light skin. As more and more African Americans make it to the middle class, more white men and African American women should find each other attractive and feel they have more in common with each other because contact between African Americans and whites should increase. In addition more African Americans would be in positions of power to affect a positive image of African Americans. Given the strong historical vestiges of racism in our society, it is questionable if we will be able to erase completely the feelings of difference between blacks and whites. I believe the gap could be closed considerably given the right conditions, i.e., greater equality.

I remember teaching a class about ten years ago at a college with which I am no longer affiliated on a Friday afternoon. It may have been the first time I ever told students about my idea that to have a preference to not interracially date could be construed by some as racist. I was trying to push their buttons. We had developed a sense of trust with each other in the classroom and a very positive climate existed for the exchange of ideas. I was about to break the trust many of them had placed in me not to personally attack them. I wanted to show that there was a possible contradiction between claiming that everyone is an individual, and thus unique, but at the same time lumping people together into racial categories.

I was well liked by many of the students at this particular institution. Colleagues told me that students respected me and loved my classes. I believe I consistently had the highest student evaluations among my sociology colleagues. The school was a small, private, liberal arts institution and expensive to attend. My audience on this Friday afternoon was largely white with perhaps one or two African American students out of about forty. As they were getting up to leave, I told them my thoughts about having a dating preference and the possibility that to have a bias against a group may mean that they were inadvertently practicing a form of racist behavior. My idea caused a great outcry of emotion and objection to my statement. No one wanted to be seen as a racist and what I had said suggested that some of them possibly were. To them, having a preference to exclude members of an entire group as a potential dating or marriage partner was just another form of individualism, a personal choice. Having a racial preference was similar to wanting to date someone with red hair instead of blonde. It was innocent and no one was harmed. I like to be accessible to my students and I received and answered a lot of e-mail that weekend.

I said something else on that Friday afternoon before they left. I indicated that if whites did not want to date African Americans that this could be construed by some as racist. But the reverse, African Americans not wanting to date whites, was not. African Americans, who did not want to date interracially, I said was evidence of prejudicial behavior, but sociologically it may not necessarily be racism, if racism is defined to mean behavior that adversely affects the quality of life of another group. That was not an idea to be pushed, that racism may not be a two-way street, right before they were leaving for the weekend, not without time to explain.

If a group has less power than another group, they cannot be racist toward the group with more power. Thus women cannot be sexist toward men, but men can and are sexist against women. Individually, yes there are powerful African Americans who can be racist, because they can personally affect the lives of others. But when racism, the ability to impede the quality of life of another, is considered from *a group perspective*, African Americans (as a group) cannot be racist and women (as a group) cannot be sexist against men because they do not have as much power as whites and men respectively. Certainly there are powerful individual African Americans and women and they have the potential to be racist and sexist, respectively, as individuals. But the above example is from a group perspective – i.e., if many members of a group express a dating or marriage preference against a minority group there can be an adverse effect on the minority group: limited social networks that could be used for jobs and the dispersal of knowledge of other resources.

Social networks are just as important, perhaps more than hard work, in order for some to be economically successful and to have access to a good quality of life. Who we know counts in our professional careers. Who we marry is also important.[41] It was against the law for African Americans to marry whites in many states up until the landmark Supreme Court decision in 1967, *Loving vs. State of Virginia*, U.S. Supreme Court, a very recent date within my lifetime and the lifetime of many of my students' parents.[42]

These laws against miscegenation were a barrier to the transference of resources between African Americans and whites.[43] They also inhibited the free flow of information via social networks that could aid or promote the ability of African Americans to procure quality jobs. I married a white female. If her parents had a family business, I could have asked them for a position in their company. Unfortunately, they do not. The point is, traditionally, it is difficult to economically discriminate against a group if you don't do it socially as well. To forbid marriage between "the races" was an important step for whites who wanted to maintain economic advantage especially in occupational niches in the workforce.

When someone has a preference it means that they see a member of a particular group as desirable or undesirable. Even if we limit our discussion of preference to physical attractiveness, we can still claim racism. It is the group in power that is able to determine who is beautiful or desirable. As a group climbs the economic and political ladders, it is reasonable to assume that social standards, e.g., standards of beauty, will change because the ascendancy of a minority group enables more members of that group to be in positions of power that could highly influence how citizens see each other.

I believe that as long as a group has a disproportionate number of its members on the bottom, then there will be negative stereotypes associated with that group. I argue that when the group moves up the ladder there will be more interaction and thus a greater sense of commonality between African Americans and whites. Specifically, there could be a blurring of caste lines similar to what has happened with gender roles as women have accrued more power. More men today than a generation ago are fine with being a house husband.

I teach not only about facts but also about racial formation processes, how issues related to race are always changing.[44] To only teach facts affirms the permanence of the status of each group, a hierarchical system whereby some groups have more power than others. I want to challenge people at their core, to suggest race is socially constructed, i.e., arbitrarily constructed so that some in our society can benefit in some way, rather than to believe race is a group of people who naturally feel a sense of "belonging" or sameness. Thus I often assert the possibility that racial categories can change in our society when circumstances warrant. I want my students to entertain the possibility, as remote as it may sound and feel, that race can be eliminated in America.

For some it may not be politically correct today to toy with the idea that race is socially constructed because it may foster contemplation about why race was created and is maintained, rather than to believe that racial affiliation is natural. According to Lerone Bennett's 1982 book, *Before the Mayflower*, at one time there was little animosity or rigid caste divisions between African Americans and whites in America. As slavery deepened, the concept of black and white was developed to fit the needs of those who benefited from slavery. The system flourished because although slavery was an economic relationship, a social relationship was necessary between African Americans and whites to justify and uphold it. This social relationship clearly delineated the status for members of each group relative to each other, where one group had a higher social status than the other. In fact race is rather new to the western lexicon, introduced within the past 500 years, at the same time as the development of capitalism.[45]

Group conflict

Preference of association is thought to be a personal choice and not thought to hinge on feelings of animosity toward members of another group. Preference to associate with someone of a particular race is not viewed by many students today as a hostile or negative action. Students believe that association is based on feelings of being comfortable with members of your own group; a sense of commonality is more rapidly felt or assumed. Since this is a major reason students give for the existence of social segregation by race on campus, it is important to look closely at why students may or may not feel they have something in common with members of a particular group.[46]

Although culture can be passed down from one generation to another, culture is always changing, and issues of class and caste influence not only the production of culture but the psychological feelings that two groups have about members of ones "own" group versus another group. Thus, as long as there are feelings of overall inequality between African Americans and whites, then there are likely to be feelings that each side is different from the other, regardless of the fact that they may or may not be culturally different. Therefore, a strong determinant of feeling different culturally may hinge on how equal members of one group feel overall relative to members of another group.

> The high degree of residential segregation imposed on blacks ensures their
> social and economic isolation from the rest of American society. ...Such
> high levels of racial isolation cannot be sustained without creating a
> profound alienation from American society and its institutions.[47]

According to Steinberg, feelings of difference that lead to conflict are really
over the acquisition and possession of resources and not differences in culture.[48]
Acquisition and possession of resources is often hindered or prevented in our
society by residential segregation. Give people access to the same resources and
more harmonious relations would probably result. Advocate real affirmative
action for 10 years so that an equal percentage of African Americans as whites
are in different occupations as per their percentages in the overall population and
then halt those affirmative action policies, and we may see far more integrated
race relations on college campuses than we currently do because each "side"
would perceive the other to be more equal. The preference to associate with
members of a particular group would not be as readily espoused.

Maintaining the Duality: Black and White

To be African American has less to do with the possibility that all African
Americans may share the same culture but more with the feeling that many
African Americans share similar life experiences relative to whites. Many
whites, who have been raised in suburban America today, as well as a growing
number of African Americans, have had little contact with the vast poverty that
now exists in urban areas. Based on the comments of my students who were
raised in the suburbs, many believe that America's streets are still paved with
gold if one works hard, has determination and keeps one's nose clean.

The images of crime in inner cities that is shown on the evening news each
night needs to be rationalized by my students, to fit a paradigm indicating that
each individual has a vast array of life choices from which to choose. Thus, the
people committing the crimes are simply seen as bad people, to be warehoused
in prison, with little thought to the possible causes, for example, the exodus of
factories to third world countries that has contributed to the level of poverty in
our country and therefore the level of violent crime particularly in urban areas.
Less attention is given to these environmental conditions by my students,
specifically the non-availability of daycare, the lack of a higher minimum wage
and the lack of access to better health care. It is easier to blame the victim, a
form of individualism, than to consider changing national policy priorities that
could affect the quality of life for a group and for all Americans.

I argue here that social interactions between members of two different races
are often negotiated in ways that are different from same-race contacts.[49]
Feelings of not having as much in common with members of the "other" race are
just as much, perhaps more so, a result of the overall inequalities that still exist

between the two races as the prevalence of cultural differences. Elimination of the ghettos, better integration of all African Americans into the economic mainstream and increased residential integration would go a long way in reducing feelings of difference between African Americans and whites.

Chapter Four
Different Generations

Although I was born in 1957, a baby boomer, I have always felt that I grew up in the shadows of World War II. I clearly did not have firsthand experience of that immense conflict. But my parents were part of the generation that had gone off to fight in that war, kept the newspaper clippings of relatives who were combat soldiers, served with honor, and returned home to fight for civil rights in the States as civilians. I think I remember as a child, in the 1960s, television commercials with images of destroyed European cities and a lone innocent child amidst the rubble, a plea for aid of some sort – perhaps for a child behind the iron curtain.

As a minority of one where I grew up, I often felt I was in constant search of allies. My best friend in elementary school was my classmate John. He lived in Penn Pines, an all white working class area adjacent to my neighborhood.[50] Others in my class, because they knew me, were friendly to me. I was one of them, "white" in a sense. My classmates usually didn't let on that I was, in reality, different. For others in my elementary school with whom I did not have a lot of contact and thus did not personally know, my race remained quite important. There were sometimes taunts and comments made when we passed in the hallway. I was very different to them. I often felt a sense of embarrassment when I was among my classmates and someone I did not know made negative comments about African Americans. I felt I had a stigma, a stain that in the eyes of some I couldn't shake.

One day on the playground when I was in the fourth grade, I was being taunted pretty severely by two kids in 5th or 6th grade. I may have been shy and didn't know how to react. John, who was white and also my best friend, interceded on my behalf. I don't remember fists being thrown but there was contact of some sort. John was a tough kid, perhaps large for his age. They never disturbed me again. Later that year I went to visit John at his house after school.

Although I was young, I had a sense of neighborhood boundaries. Like my own middle class neighborhood, the area where John lived, solid working class and blue collar, did not have one single African American. Perhaps touching on a stereotype, John's neighborhood seemed tougher than mine. Even today when I drive through this area I remember how I felt when I was young. The only difference now is that there is great diversity in that area. I never thought that African American families would ever live there but now some do. Perhaps my optimism is tempered by the fact that this area and where I grew up is now considered to be part of the older suburbs, one of the inner ring suburbs closest to Philadelphia. As African Americans have pushed out many whites have left presumably to the deeper suburbs or out of metro America altogether.[51]

I had visited John before. But on this occasion, a couple doors before I reached my destination, I was approached and taunted by a group of four or five kids, some of whom I recognized from my elementary school, in grades other than my own. They blocked my path, spit a couple times on my bike, and generally harassed me by asking me why I was in their neighborhood. They didn't attack me physically but I remember feeling outnumbered and thinking they were capable of actually striking me if I "talked back." The only recourse was to simply wait until they were done.

While these kids were taunting me, I noticed John start to come out of his house. I also saw his mother peek outside above his head. She quickly pulled John back inside. My only hope to escape these kids was now gone, safely tucked away in his house. I never forgot that incident. John's mother, perhaps sensing I was an "unwanted" by the neighborhood bullies and unable to resist the will of the masses, pulled her son to safety.

The feeling of threat from a perceived outside group

The area where I grew up, a narrow paved road that consisted of eight houses, four on each side with access to wooded areas nearby, was solidly middle class. But my quality of life was different from the other kids on that road. I didn't experience the same circumstances as they did. Even at a young age I remember being more guarded about what I did and where I went. I could not isolate my own living conditions from the outside world or even from images or stereotypes that existed in America at that time. The concept of race, although it may not have manifested itself or originated in my immediate environment, affected my daily intimate social interactions with my friends. My immediate world was interwoven with a larger context, American society, in ways that I did not fully understand nor did my classmates.

Although my suburb was located very near Philadelphia, back in the early 1960s I remember running through corn fields in my neighborhood as well as seeing a vegetable stand in another area with produce I assume had been grown locally. As the 1960s came to a close, many more houses and three or four large apartment complexes were built in the surrounding areas. My once seemingly isolated road became very crowded in a short period of time. Even at a young age I remember a feeling of loss. I do have concern for the quality of life that my parents, who still live there, are able to have now that there is far more congestion than even twenty years ago. The physical qualities of my suburb, open spaces, seem to resemble Philadelphia more and more with each passing decade.

Pressure from below

The interconnections between race and class are apparent to me. It is intriguing to note that periods of increased competition for jobs have soured race relations between African Americans and whites. At the height of industrialization, the late 1800s and early 1900s, millions of Southern and Eastern European immigrants flooded America and found jobs in factories, a huge if not dominant sector of the economy at that time. Although Southern and Eastern Europeans may not have been racist when they arrived,[52] it can be argued that being racist against African Americans after they arrived was to make sure that they, Southern and Eastern Europeans, maintained a foothold in the factories at the expense of African Americans who remained in rural America.[53] Relations between African Americans and whites are often felt to be linear, progressing in a straight line from bad to better; an argument can also be made that race relations have been curvilinear thus with ebbs and flows because of varying situational contexts when whites have felt more or less threatened by African Americans for jobs.

Attending college today is not the novelty that it may once have been only a generation ago when one had the choice of working in a white collar job or making a good living as a member of the working class. Out of all of the 70 or so classmates from my 6th grade (there were three 6th grade teachers), my final year in elementary school, I was the only one to obtain a doctorate although many went to college. I don't think they felt the same urgency that I did to attend graduate school. Unlike many of my classmates, I knew from my earliest days in elementary school I was going to go to college. For some of my classmates there seemed to be alternative paths to happiness or life satisfaction, making a living, rather than attending college and certainly instead of going on and getting a doctorate.

Socially it was easier for them. Thus, in planning a future, I don't think the absence of graduate school credentials was seen as limiting or preventing one from leading the "good life." Whereas I felt it was important, still do, to have a graduate degree in order to have more life choices in terms of where to live and whom I would have contact with in the future.

Perhaps as a result of a decline in good paying working class jobs, one out of two Americans today have stepped foot inside a college classroom, have at least taken a class, at some point in their life. The fact that so many people now rely on a college education today as a ticket to more economic security may have increased the backlash against affirmative action from a group that supported it a generation earlier, the white middle class.[54] Competition to remain in the middle class may feel much keener today than a generation earlier. Battles are not being fought in the streets in the form of "race wars," as they once were when the white working class was still in urban America and needed to prevent occupational and residential incursions by African Americans, but in very middle class "ways," i.e., through the courts, legislation and in electoral politics, to reverse policies perceived now to be "reverse discrimination."

Because working class whites had been more firmly entrenched within the mainstream of the economy, they worked in the factories in the early part of the twentieth century, they were in a much better position to make the move to the newly forming middle class suburbs in the second half of the century than other groups who were economically more marginalized such as African Americans. A disproportionate number of African Americans were intentionally kept marginalized in the twentieth century while working class whites maintained a secure economic foothold and were able to move in large numbers into the middle class.[55]

The middle class today is still, compared to the lower and upper class, more liberal in social and political attitudes. But the pressures from the working class to join the middle class will continue to increase rather than abate and continue to push members within this stratum, the middle class, to use race as a rallying cry. More claims of reverse discrimination are likely to occur.

Open discussions of reverse discrimination were not as tolerated a generation ago as they seem to be today. Coincidently, the working class was stronger then. An individual engaged in charging that whites were under attack would not have been taken seriously and that individual in some cases would have been ridiculed and thought to be racist, and if running for a public office, seen as possibly unfit.

Neo-conservative movements today have not invoked these feelings of reverse discrimination in a vacuum, but have taken advantage of changes in the overall nature of the economy. Thus we are more likely to see a hardening of race relations in middle class America in the future rather than a lessening of racial boundaries, regardless of how many interracial marriages occur. Thus it can be argued that it isn't the number of interracial marriages, thus biracial children, that determines racial boundaries, but the overall sense of competition African Americans and whites feel relative to each other.

Practicing multiculturalism will still be the order of the day and will be seen as a way to bridge the divide. But at the same time practicing multiculturalism will represent the presence of the divide and will reaffirm that there are indeed racial boundaries in this country. Thus, on the one hand, multiculturalism is needed in order to keep good race relations and to believe that America is a color blind society. But, more and more middle class liberals will continue to embrace multiculturalism while at the same time claim to be hurt by discriminatory policies against whites. Multiculturalism, while it stands for progressive race relations through an acknowledgement of perceived cultural differences, does not necessarily signify that more structural changes are in order such as integrated neighborhoods, occupational integration or better schools.

The splintering of race but within the framework of black and white

Although I am very fair, when growing up, I was always considered to be African American by whites and African Americans. In the classes that I teach today I have been asked by both African American and white students who I am racially. My light skin presents a mystery for some much more so than I can recall when I was younger or when I was in college. Students seem to want to know who they are dealing with in the classroom. There is still a strong sense that there is a black and a white race that is separate from each other. Students are apt to label people "mixed race" today but they still see and feel each end of the spectrum.

Because of my age and how and what I experienced when growing up, I do feel a sense of irritation in my classroom when someone asks me who I am. It shows a naiveté about American history. On the one hand some may see movement toward a new racial category of "mixed" as overall progress in race relations. But it is also possible to argue that racial lines have been drawn tighter and people are anxious to know who is who, to be able to clearly define who is on what side of the playing field.

White parents, according to my students, still are not comfortable with the appropriation of so-called ghetto culture by their children. For African Americans, my automatic inclusion as a member of the club became somewhat more nebulous beginning with the rise of the Black Power movement and continues today with an emphasis on multiculturalism rather than assimilation. Under assimilation I was definitely not white. With multiculturalism, perhaps used by some to splinter the race categories into a third, my identity is more ambiguous today because my skin is so fair.

> The derisive term "high yaller" indicates that very light mulattoes have often been considered illegitimate and trashy if they cannot demonstrate respectable family connections. Although this implies a rejection of the

one-drop rule, the meaning seems usually to be that such persons are indeed black, but very "low-down" blacks. Similarly, since the 1960s, light mulattoes who have been put on the defensive by vigorous expressions of black pride have been made to feel they must take pains to emphasize their respectability and their blackness or they will barely be tolerated in the black community.[56]

I am of another generation when black meant that even the tiniest amount dictated that one was to be considered, and considered oneself, proudly to be only African American. I am from another time period that stretches back prior to the modern-day civil rights movement, when Black meant Black regardless of how much. My ancestors, especially on my father's side, were all light, many with wavy hair. My father, who could probably pass, was not allowed to live in the dorms at Penn State in the 1940s because people knew who he was, a "Colored" man.

To compensate light skin people may feel a need to prove they "belong" more so today than a generation ago. Of course a lot depends on where one is raised. It is much easier to feel a sense of belonging if one is raised with other African Americans and can thus develop a greater sense of awareness that is necessary in order to counter the continued bombardment of negative stereotypes that exist about African Americans in suburban white enclaves. Otherwise, growing up in an all white situation, although the result can include many positive social experiences and long lasting friendships with whites, may make it quite difficult to develop the same level of positive self esteem and self image.

Your friends who are white may appreciate you for who you are as an individual but their friends, assuming they are white, aren't always going to make the same assumptions. You are either invisible to their friends, thus you aren't black, you are treated as white and thus you can make the same bad jokes about African Americans as they, go along to get along. Or you are "black" to their friends and thus there is a great lag time, lack of spontaneity as they try to feel you out and you they to see how safe socially interacting with them is going to be.

Dating becomes a challenge since one has to negotiate and manage possible perceptions at every turn, those that white parents still may have about being too black, or those that African American women may have about being "too close" to white maleness, i.e., African American men who have light skin. As Victor pointed out in the *Color of Fear*, whites still feel more at ease around him than they do his mother who has a darker complexion than he.[*]

---

[*] I am reminded of an incident that an almost newly minted doctoral student recently had when he was teaching a class. He lectured a great deal about the intersections of race, class and gender. In one of his classes two white students complained to their respective advisors that he was racist against whites. In reality all he had done was talk about race, a subject for many whites that is still taboo – i.e., they have been raised in an environment

The social turmoil of the 60s produced different results for each group. African Americans defined more clearly "who was in" and "who was out." Previous to the 60s, it was lighter shade African Americans who were prominent in African American communities. After the 60s, it was African Americans who were darker who were able to achieve prominence for the first time in history in large numbers.[57] Black Power also meant that African Americans would be in the vanguard, ahead of white allies, in the fight against racism just as women and not men would be in the vanguard to fight sexism. Any other arrangement was seen as a recapitulation to the subordination of African Americans and women to the majority.

Lighter-skin African Americans, especially men, during the 1960s were felt by some African Americans as not automatically worthy of trust. It was important to be African American and not an Oreo cookie, black on the outside but white on the inside. Many white liberals felt alienated and ceased active participation in the fight for African American equality.

I do think for African Americans like myself who grew up in all white neighborhoods, achieving or finding an identity was very hard. To be light has made finding an identity extra hard. Even though my parents were fair they were able to have significant contact with African Americans when growing up which enabled them to shape who they were, to see themselves more clearly. Being light and in an all residential white situation only encouraged the active denial of blackness on some occasions, "I really am one of you. Please accept me," I might have wanted to say to my white classmates. Consider the experiences of the following sociologist who wrote:

> Though I was ideologically committed to and intellectually convinced of black equality – indeed, proud to claim my African-American heritage – I did not have everyday experience with African Americans or other people of color. This lack of experience had retarded my comfort with myself and hampered my ability to move among different groups with ease. The gaze of a few white classmates felt like a spotlight, and I was paralyzed, feeling much of the time as though I were on a stage without a script.

Even in the early years of her college experience, there was a sense of discomfort for her:

---

not to talk about race and to do so is seen and felt as racist. The instructor talked to those in the administration about the incident. When it was divulged that one of his parents was white, there was almost an audible sigh of relief from one administrator. Since he had a white parent it was thought that he could not be racist against whites.

Choosing to sit at the black table in the dining center at Haverford was a less comfortable option for me than transplanting myself to a place where no one knew me. I applied to several HBCUs as an exchange student for the fall semester of my junior year, was accepted at Spelman College, and arrived in Atlanta in August 1984 for orientation .

Nonetheless, Spelman gave me a security with myself as a black person: I saw such a wide range of African Americans that I began to conceive of blackness as inclusive of a variety of experiences, I began to appreciate that many of my black classmates back at Haverford, who had come from mostly black environments, must have felt extreme dislocation.*[58]

For whites, the liberal 60s also meant the expansion of the range of acceptable social behavior such as premarital sex, cohabitation, and more, values that are now firmly embraced by many in the middle class. The development of these more liberal values coincided with the movement of whites to the suburbs and residential separation from African Americans. The majority of African Americans by the end of the 1960s were living in urban areas in contrast to whites who were now over represented in the suburbs in comparison to other areas of the country.

A cultural milieu was developing in suburban America in the 1970s that was different from a culture dominated by ethnic-group politics that had existed in urban America. Liberal values began to emphasize equality based on individualism or "pull yourself up by your own bootstraps." A new tension developed between those who still wanted to advocate for the rights of the group and those who only wanted to place emphasis on the individual. The former tended to believe in affirmative action policies. Those who placed primacy in the rights of the individual began to claim that affirmative action policies were reverse discrimination. In the 1980s the charge of reverse racism grew louder and louder.

African Americans disproportionately experience lower wages and greater unemployment. Some students who take my classes have been raised to believe that racism is when someone speaks ill of someone else or treats someone differently because of the color of their skin. I tell my students, that although this behavior may still exist, this is the racism of yesterday. The new racism is not being able to recognize that a disproportionate number of African Americans are experiencing a lower quality life. Solutions therefore are required in the form of new national policy initiatives rather than placing blame on the individual for the ills of society.

---

* I do not mean to imply that the experiences of the sociologist quoted here are identical to mine. I only imply that what she wrote felt similar to what I experienced on numerous occasions.

It isn't clear what it means to be liberal today. One can be in favor of cohabiting but against affirmative action policies. Both positions, in favor of cohabitation and affirmative action, were seen as solidly liberal not very long ago. Americans seem to be suffering from fractured political identities today in comparison to more consistent intellectual and emotional paradigms they pushed and felt about thirty years ago.

Chapter Five
"Where did all the hippies go?"

I was too young for Woodstock, but I wish I had been there for some unknown reason. I do not mean to imply that my politics are liberal or conservative, but there was something about that time period for me in a very romantic way that seemed to signify a deep sense of community among baby boomers. There was a belief among some politicians that social problems could be overcome if we all worked together to make a better society.[59]

In spirit I am a hippie, although most hippies would probably be identified as white - Jimi Hendrix and Richie Havens were exceptions. Still today I listen to music that I associate with that era. Perhaps I am a closet flower child who would like to turn back the clock in San Francisco to that time period when that city attracted so many young people who wore flowers in their hair that signified to many a sense of commonality.

I sometimes see a stray Volkswagen Beetle or camper with stick-on neon-like flowers but they are few and far between, usually a college student today has stuck them to his or her car because they struck a positive aesthetic cord. Those car owners that I have talked to are aware of the 60s, but they do not feel they are making some sort of societal statement nor do they feel they are part of a new generation that stands in contrast to an older one. Occasionally there are some bell bottom pants that are worn by the young today. Thicker and wider belts seem to be making a return as well and women are wearing shorter skirts, also reminiscent of the mini skirt. I doubt students, who dress like this, are even aware that they may be dressing in a style similar to forty years ago. I wonder if students even have a sense that they represent a generation. Or, do they feel a sense of separation from each other that obliterates such feelings? The latter seems to be more likely.

Although students see me as someone who is older and have told me so, they do not seem to have a joie de vivre or unity that makes them seem as one. Often they tell me they are more liberal and more tolerant than older people like me. Indeed on surveys they are more tolerant of interracial marriages and homosexuality than a generation ago. But their tolerance is couched in a deep sense of separation or disconnectedness from others, "if they aren't bothering me, let them do whatever they want," I can hear students say. This is a live-and-let-live approach in a world that is often viewed as dog-eat-dog, competitive, do what you need to do to survive and seek pleasure when possible.

I find it strange that the music of the 60s, music that I still listen to like Dylan, Cream, Velvet Underground, or Crosby Stills Nash and Young, has been appropriated by certain media outlets as lead-ins to talk shows that preach not community but a heightened sense of separation from each other that borders on an ideology of survival of the fittest. There is nothing wrong with going down this path, but it does not seem to be tempered with alternative viewpoints, those that discuss a sense of community and the sharing of the social problems that plague our fellow Americans. In our society today what occurs in your life is viewed as a result of "you only have yourself to praise or blame," or "we all have choices." It is so odd to walk past dorm windows to hear all of this seemingly radical music from the 60s and then listen to students who listen to the music because it sounds good and make no connections at all to the context when it was first heard by their parents' generation. The music has been made innocent.

I was too young to be at Mexico City to witness two African American athletes Jimmy Heinz and Tommy Smith, raise their black-gloved hands and bow their heads on the podium when the national anthem was played, in protest of the treatment of African Americans. I may not agree with what they did but I know they spoke to a wider audience in America, one that seemed very concerned about various issues unlike today where there seems to be an atomization and disconnect of Americans from each other. Black Power movements and ideas associated with multiculturalism would become very meaningful to me about 6th grade because they exposed how different the quality of life was for African Americans compared to whites. These movements and ideas probably held less value for my classmates and neighbors since they potentially called for change in the status quo.[60]

I remember the day the headline of the Michigan Daily announced that John Lennon had been shot. I walked into an early morning sociology class. This was a rather interesting class and I have not heard of one like it since, at least not in sociology. It was about the effectiveness of various military fighting units. It was thus a class not about why nations go to war but how effectively various military personnel and branches fought when they were at war, especially when they were in combat. The class was taught by an African American woman who loved her course and subject matter. I walked into the classroom that day and she was sobbing in the arms of a white male. John Lennon had been shot and died. Later that day on the "Diag," a common area at the center of the campus at the University of Michigan, a couple hundred students stood in silence. It was an overcast day. I remember weaving my way through people who stood eerily motionless. When students play his music today, for some the political messages are not recognized.

Where have the liberals gone? Occasionally I meet students who seem to be in that vain, but they don't connect the dots as fluidly as the hippies of the 60s seemingly did. For many students grassroots organizing to solve social problems is not considered or seen as effective. Tuition hikes occur and rarely is there a student who makes his or her voice heard. In private they may say something to a friend, or a teacher, or in class there may be a day when they will feel they have had enough and vent, but it rarely goes further. I have a strong feeling that they are so concerned about their own survival that organizing for the survival of others is a tough thing to do, seen as too risky.

In the 1960s, the economy was good and jobs were readily available especially for college grads. There was a sense that one could get by and still survive. Students today have a greater sense of urgency, not knowing where they will need to go to make a living but feeling pressure that the world of work is rough out there. Many are quite frightened about what they will be doing after graduation. A bachelor's degree just doesn't go very far today.

As a teacher I do feel it is unethical to push a political agenda in the classroom. I suppose if I were a teacher back in the late 1960s and my students pushed very liberal ideas I would feel compelled to show more conservative ideas for a sense of balance. Given that I rarely hear ideas considered by some to be liberal today, such as consideration of an increase in social spending, I feel it is my job to point out this perspective so there is a sense of balance in the classroom.

I remember Gil Scott-Heron's song, "The Revolution Will Not Be Televised," Marvin Gaye's song, "What's Going On?" and James Brown's song, "Say It Loud (I'm Black and I'm Proud)." Today there is rap, often with a political message as well. But who hears the message? Some do. But many, especially whites and some African Americans, do not. They like the music but do not see any connection to real circumstances, or how these circumstances may have an impact on their own lives. It is like a genre of music has been pulled from the air without any basis for its possible origin. This is okay, but again, Americans do not seem to be approaching social problems from the standpoint that we are all affected by these social problems. Instead we are individuals only concerned about ourselves.

Because of the fear of crime in urban America, these spaces are now off limits to millions of Americans. Entire geographic areas of America, cities, have been in a sense cordoned off from those who do not live there out of fear. Hundreds of years of rich American history complete with decaying architecturally wonderful buildings are being lost in some areas.

The sense of disconnect from our fellow rural citizens is also profound. There is a greater incidence of divorce, partner abuse, teenage pregnancy there than in suburban areas. Our politicians seem less willing today to consider that the origins of many social problems may be connected to the loss of manufacturing jobs similar to what has happened in urban America.

One might expect a heightened sense of atomization in suburban areas. More people have resources in these areas than in urban and rural areas thus there may be feelings of competition with each other to acquire even more. A heightened sense of atomization has seeped into urban and rural America as well. In urban America there is a sense of toughness and survival of the fittest.[61] The same is evident in rural America although it often does not play out with the same sense of brazen violence. But certainly the idea and feeling of survival of the fittest is present there as well.

How much has really changed?

When the jobs, as well as the urban working class moved to the suburbs, many of their children were able to break away from traditional lifestyles. Many became the first in their family to go off to college. Not only men but women went off to college. They were away from parental control where they could experiment with alternative types of behavior such as premarital sex and living together. Having a college degree further challenged the ability of parents to replicate their own lifestyle through their kids because their children were less dependent on them to make a living. An education gave the children more occupational choices as well as places to live. Perhaps the show that typified the new changes the most was "All in the Family." Mike and Gloria initially lived with her parents, Archie and Edith, while Mike was going to school. As the show entered the final years, Mike and Gloria finally moved out and Michael is offered a job three thousand miles away in California. The new middle class, typified by Mike and Gloria, has mobility. A challenge to traditional gender roles was also initiated given that large numbers of women were subsequently able to enter the middle class and put forth voices for change during this time period.

Middle class jobs operated differently from working class jobs. Promotion through seniority was not always guaranteed. Membership in a particular ethnic group no longer boosted one's chances of securing employment in specific occupations as it may have done for the children's parents in urban America during the factory time period.[62] Attending college and thus acquiring credentials became more important for the new middle class offspring. Given the rules of the new economy, it became more difficult to rationalize keeping women and minorities out of mainstream occupations if they had the same credentials as members of the majority.

Many of the children of the working class suburbanites of the 1950s were perceived as members of the counterculture in the 1960s, the hippies. To older generations, who were more working class at that time (because the middle class was still developing), they seemed to be a coherent uniform mass out to cripple the values of their parents' generation. But what seemed like a unified generation of young people rebelling against the norms of society can now be viewed using a different perspective.

Perhaps they were not as radical as many suspected. Perhaps it was just the growing pains of a society that was moving from an industrial society, that emphasized conformity of behavior among its large working class population, to a post industrial society that called for less conformity, because the American population became more middle class thus more mobility was needed. Perhaps alternative lifestyles flourished not only because people were less able to develop the deep sense of community that could push conformity of values, but also because post industrial society depended on a labor force that was more able to adjust to new situations domestically and globally. Therefore the sedentary working class neighborhoods of an industrial error accompanied by a particular type of social behavior that defined what it meant to be a man and a woman in very traditional ways became out dated and in a sense not very healthy to the expanded labor needs of the new economy. The door also opened for more interracial marriages, another break with traditional behavior.

The young generation that seemed as though it spoke with one voice during the 1960s in reaction to the seemingly stifling values of their parents, may not have been as unified as many suspected but was simply reacting to the growing pains of our nation. People wanted to "do their own thing" express themselves in unique albeit seemingly rebellious ways, but was this not good for the economy in the long run? Many of the hippies were anti-materialistic but in the end came back into the fold, became productive workers and it can be argued spawned the "me" generation of the 1980s. During the 1980s we had conservative politics but they were coupled with behavior that was much more liberal than that of the 1950s, and there was also an emphasis on materialism and consumerism. It seems to me that the counter cultural movements of the 1960s catapulted our nation into a post industrial time period by diversifying our social behavior something very needed for a new post industrial global economy.

Is there a loss of community today? Perhaps the middle class never had it but only working class cultures had it, albeit often with bad results, i.e., to keep undesirables out and to force its members to conform to certain types of acceptable behavior. Although the middle class is larger today than a couple generations ago, the emphasis on individualism, "pull yourself up by your own bootstraps," is blinding. Because the poor are isolated from other classes, the upper and middle classes are unable to see and understand the many social problems that disproportionately affect millions of Americans in both urban and rural areas. There is also a tendency to see a culture of poverty among the poor and to therefore "blame the victim." Feelings of racial difference between the haves and have nots further impedes an understanding of the life experiences of those in other classes.

What should be done?

A unified movement of white and black social activists was never destined to survive the 1960s given that each group lived and experienced life from different perspectives derived from logistically two different areas, urban and suburban.[63] The social milieu that many African Americans who still reside in urban regions are now exposed is quite different than the social milieu for many whites who now reside in suburban areas. I believe that how African Americans and whites today see themselves and each other is dependent on environmental circumstances, i.e., urban versus suburban areas. Each group is engaged in something akin to impression management, playing out expected roles, while interacting with each other in ways that are heavily influenced by the overall circumstances each group faces. These circumstances give rise to feelings of difference between the two groups.

Middle class individualism can be seen as an ideology that legitimizes class position. Although there are exceptions it is far easier for someone born into the middle class to "remain" in the middle class than for someone born poor to move into the middle class. A heightened individualism as a dominant ideology masks the sociological patterns of behavior and educational outcomes – i.e., the higher the social class the higher one usually scores on standardized tests, is more likely to attend college and to stay in college longer. Even though there are many African Americans who now reside in the suburbs, it is hard for whites or African Americans on college campuses to overcome feelings of difference deeply affected by what I believe to be the overall relationship between African Americans and whites outside the walls of academia: residential segregation, lack of social contact and under representation in numerous occupations.[64]

A new post industrial economy, with an emphasis on global competition and thus global awareness, required that a sizable proportion of Americans in the 1960s rebel against the conformity of the previous generation. Many African Americans have been able to join the ranks of the middle class. Many more remain marginalized and thus are dependent on jobs that do not pay living wages.

As indicated in a later chapter on dating on college campuses, the social constraints of yesterday that inhibited communication between the two groups are still at work today on our nation's campuses given the differences in overall geographic and economic isolation of each group relative to the other off campus. Very different lifestyles are thus experienced by members of each group.[65] To influence how group members feel about each other requires changing the overall relationship of each group relative to the other off campus.[66][67]

The Need for Affirmative Action

Affirmative action policies fostered an expansion of the African American middle class. Many subsequently moved to the suburbs away from urban areas, thereby increasing the concentration of poor in many urban census tracts. The result has been an increase in separation of the African American middle, and upper classes, from the lower.[68] The African American lower class has become more isolated from the hub of the economy that is now located in the suburbs. Because of this spatial separation there has been a reduction in access to viable social networks that lead to good jobs. Separation by class, as well as by race, remains an important deterrent to mobility for African Americans, particularly those in the lower classes.[69]

To be white and poor and to live in urban America is different than to be African American and poor.[70] Royster wrote the following:

> The implications for black men are devastating. Despite having unprecedented access to the same preparatory institution [for example, training as an electrician] as their white peers, black males could not effectively use the institutional connection to establish successful trade entry. Moreover, segregation in multiple social arenas, beyond schools, all but precluded the possibility of network overlaps among working-class black and white men...
>
> Again and again, the white men I spoke with described opportunities that had landed in their laps, not as the result of outstanding achievements or personal characteristics, but rather as the result of the assistance of older white neighbors, brothers, family friends, teachers, uncles, fathers, and sometimes mothers, aunts, and girlfriends...
>
> My systematic examination of the experiences of these fifty matched young men leads me to conclude that the blue-collar labor market does not function as a market in the classic sense. No pool of workers presents itself, offering sets of skills and work values that determine who gets matched with the most and least desirable opportunities. Rather, older men who recruit, hire, and fire young workers choose those with whom they are comfortable or familiar. Visible hands trump the "invisible hand" – and norms of racial exclusivity passed down from generation to generation in American cities continues to inhibit black men's entry into the better skilled jobs in the blue-collar sector.

...And given persistent patterns of segregation – equivalent to an American apartheid, according to leading sociologists – there remain few incentives for white men to adopt young black men into informal, neighborhood – generated networks. As a result, occupational apartheid reigns in the sector that has always held the greatest potential for upward mobility, or just basic security, for modestly educated Americans.

...The enduring power of segregated networks in the blue – collar trades is as responsible as segregated neighborhoods for the existence of extremely poor and isolated black communities and of the disproportionately black and male prison population – in fact, more so.[71]

It is more difficult for African Americans to make "the jump" into the suburbs than it is for whites.[72] More negative stereotypes related to being poor, African American and from "the ghetto" can be applied to all African Americans in ways that can severely hamper residential, social networking and economic mobility for African Americans who strive to make it up the ladder. Poor whites are not faced with this additional burden. When whites acquire money, there are more positive social images associated with success and working hard that are transferred to them and fewer to African Americans because of the overall image our society has of whites compared to African Americans. The "system" serves to push whites up and push African Americans down. How we think about members of a particular group does have an effect on their life chances, i.e., social networking processes and where one lives and works.

In order to tackle urban poverty, thus to reduce feelings of a racial divide, we should strive to create mixed race and income neighborhoods as well as quality schools associated with these neighborhoods. More integrated residential patterns would serve to foster more integrated social networks and a greater availability of role models to children and teenagers. I support equality for each race relative to the other in order to lessen feelings of difference between members of each group, i.e., an equal percentage of African Americans and whites who are in the upper, middle and lower class relative to their percentage in the overall population. This would result in less emphasis placed on race and greater feelings of commonality between African Americans and whites.[73]

A lack of economic integration, residential segregation and segregated social networks has fostered the following social circumstances:

1. Strong feelings of separation exist between African Americans and whites – social behavior on our nation's campuses is evidence of the divide.[74] It is fashionable for middle-class whites to appropriate "black culture" without thinking about the overall situation African Americans face especially in

ghettos.[75] Both groups may actually share aspects of a similar culture but interpret it differently.

2. Current African American resources, e.g. income levels, do not provide the same access to corresponding resources compared to whites.[76] An African American family lives in a neighborhood with an average income less than the average income of a neighborhood where a white family with a comparable income lives. Logan and Oakley wrote:

> Separate neighborhoods also continue to be unequal. One of the major costs of residential segregation is that minorities live in poorer neighborhoods with less resources than do whites with comparable incomes. [77]

> The average black elementary student in a metropolitan school district attended a school where 64.3% of classmates were poor. This contrasts with 29.6% in the average white student's school.[78]

Social networks for African Americans do not provide the same quality of life as the social networks created by whites. Since test scores often correlate with the level of resources a family has, African American children score lower on standardized tests even when compared to white children from families with comparable income levels.[79] African American resources thus do not "buy" as much.

It is quite difficult to do research on race and to assume that class can be held constant because of these differences between the strength of what I would call the "black dollar" versus the "white dollar." There is still the tendency to conclude that African Americans of all classes are more prone to a *culture of poverty*-type explanation, i.e., do not try hard to succeed, without taking into consideration that African Americans of all classes do not have access to an equal share of resources as their white counterparts of the same class.

3. In *Code of the Street: Decency, Violence, and the Moral Life of the Inner City* (1990), Elijah Anderson wrote about a culture that exists in some areas of urban American that are poor and African American – one that is based on being tough and physical. It is perpetuated not only by a lack of jobs but also the non-existence of middle class men and women who could be role models and provide substantial resources to the community.

4. African Americans and whites, because of economic inequality, experience the world differently. African Americans are more aware of their surroundings given the lack of representation in proportion to their numbers, in businesses and social settings, than whites. There exists a sense of relative deprivation between African Americans and whites to each other.

The existence of urban ghettos, and poor rural white areas, is keeping Americans from recognizing a common history among its citizens. Jill Quadegno, in *The Color of Welfare* (1994), argued that those in power used race to keep Americans divided after World War II in order to avoid spending tax dollars on social programs. Western European citizens had more success uniting within respective countries and thus created a more robust safety net (e.g., universal health care and guaranteed family income programs). The concept of race fostered a deep divide in our society that splintered potential solidarity among the American population.

Today the concept of a *model minority* emphasizes that some groups more than others have better values, are more family oriented and are more motivated. Although it is often not blatantly stated, the concept of a model minority is implied and reinforced through images in the media of urban unrest and crime, that African Americans are not a model minority. We may not be playing the race card directly but it seems the message is there.

Inequality and Whiteness Studies

Scholars who do work in whiteness studies emphasize that whites do have a group or racial identity. George Herbert Mead made a distinction between different forms of socialization processes, the *particular other* and the *generalized other*.[80] The particular other emphasizes what we learn from those who have raised us, such as our parents. The generalized other is what we learn from our society, the overall impressions we have and the stereotypes we know. I think they are equally powerful. I know of many students who have courageously thrown away the values of prejudice and bigotry espoused by their parents and their communities and adopted more egalitarian values.

The influence of our community on the behavior of individuals is often overlooked today as many of our politicians have tried to turn back the clock by placing total emphasis on the family. Emphasis is placed on our parents and those individuals immediately around us to explain social behavior. African American residential segregation affects access to a higher quality of life and resources. Shapiro wrote:

> ...In 2000 three-quarters of blacks lived in highly segregated communities. Residential segregation persists at high levels, and it remains a powerful force undermining the well-being of blacks, who are concentrated in communities with weak public services like hospitals, transportation, police and fire protection, with decreased housing appreciation, and with inferior schools.
>
> The residential color line is the key feature distinguishing African Americans from all other groups in the United States...Since middle-class black families tend to share neighborhoods with more poor people

than white middle-class families do, and since they more often live near and share schools with lower-class blacks, middle-class black students continue to face educational disadvantages.

...The evidence strongly suggests that segregation persists because of ongoing racial discrimination in real estate and mortgage markets, the persistence of white prejudice, and the discriminatory impact of public policies like local zoning decisions and the isolation of public housing....

Residential segregation is the linchpin of American race relations because so much else flows through community dynamics[81]

Without healthy neighborhoods and access to significant role models, even the best parenting is challenged and teenagers become vulnerable to the ills of the streets. More substantial cross-racial contact needs to occur in order to provide maximum access to resources.

In my exploratory study of parents in a housing project a number of years ago, I met very few parents who did not express a deep love for their children and a desire for a happy and successful future for them. Unfortunately, poverty-strewn communities that are unable to foster access to health care, after school programs, part time jobs for teens, and daycare often negate the best plans parents have for their offspring. Too often we place blame on parents and neglect to examine the influence of communities on families. Love for our children can only conquer so much.

Interpersonal contact with members of a different race does not necessarily serve to eliminate stereotypes held about another group. One can have numerous *good* experiences with people of the "other" race but yet still be against policies that could potentially affect race relations for the better by improving the quality of life for African Americans.

Stereotypes can be produced not only by a lack of contact between two groups, but also by different life circumstances, respectively. Examples of different life circumstances include: living in areas that are more urban than suburban and a lack of occupation integration.[82] The existence of ghettos, which are impoverished racially segregated areas, must therefore be eliminated if we truly desire a *generalized other*, our community, to be free of prejudicial and discriminatory influences. Macro structures do affect how members of one group think about members of another group and influence our everyday interpersonal relationships with each other.[83]

The establishment of an African American middle class opened the dam to the production of more positive stereotypes associated with being African American to compete with those still extant negative ones. It isn't contact between the races but the positive perceptions or stereotypes of each other that lead to increased feelings of commonality. The definition of race may have less to do with physical or even cultural differences today between African Americans and whites, but more to do with the feelings of difference often contingent on the two groups living in spatially separate areas, not sharing social networks and the overall quality of life one group experiences relative to the other.

Section III

Social Systems, Identity and Interaction

Chapter Six
Situational contexts

When I was an undergraduate I lived in a house owned by a fraternity whose members were predominantly white. I was initially not a member of the fraternity, but over a period of time, I became friends with some of the men and was subsequently encouraged to join. I think what stood out for me during the short time I was a member was the fact that the fraternity was sex segregated. I found this to be somewhat awkward if not baffling given that the members of this fraternity greatly enjoyed talking with and being with women.

I felt separation of the sexes produced a wide and unnecessary psychological chasm between men and women. Women became "the other." Although women were in a sense to be cherished and given great respect, they were perceived and experienced in very different ways than men, who were part of the male-to-male social interaction. My liberal middle class values made me question quite deeply how long I wanted to remain in an all-male environment. Even at that age and at that time period, the mid 1970s, I was familiar enough with my own feminism to know that having respect for women and wanting equality were very different issues, that respect was not the same or nearly as important as equality.

Looking back it occurred to me that this was a situation where structure had an impact on the relationship between the sexes, affecting how men thought of women and the nature of the friendships and more serious relationships that may have developed between Greek men and women.* If the men of that fraternity

---

* I do believe it is important to distinguish between predominantly white fraternities and sororities and those that are predominantly African American. Race, as a variable, does

had had more everyday contact with women as equals in the same social organization, and thus both sexes would have been members, the gender roles often associated with each sex would have been challenged and both men and women would have felt they had more choices in terms of how they wanted to lead their lives. There would have been a greater sense of bonding between the two sexes and a subsequent blurring of ascribed gender roles. In a sense the men of the fraternity were victims of an organizational structure that had been in existence on college campuses for hundreds of years. Only recently, within the past four or five decades, have institutions of higher learning admitted women. If I had a chance to do it over again, I would not have joined an all-male fraternity, not because of a dislike of others in the fraternity (I did have some positive experiences), but because my values are different.[84] Although I kept in touch with some members, I left the fraternity to live elsewhere after only one semester as a member.

I subsequently chose to join a living situation that was co-ed and cooperative. In my new cooperative house, both sexes shared cooking meals and cleaning. There were about forty people associated with my house and another 600 spread throughout the campus in other houses. All of the houses were connected under a shared-governance organization. We hired staff who were non-students to oversee the day-to-day running of the houses. We, the residents, who were mostly students, were owners of the houses. We made the decisions, even to hire and fire the staff. In each house we shared work such as cooking and cleaning. We pooled our money together and hired outside contractors when necessary to do maintenance on existing structures.

There was much more social contact between the two sexes in this living situation than there was at the fraternity. While the men at the fraternity talked very openly about having sex with women in very graphic and sometimes lewd ways, they had limited encounters with women. On the other hand, there was rarely if ever such talk in the cooperative living situation, but there was probably more intimacy between the sexes. Again this is a case where one type of structure fostered a particular relationship between men and women than another.*

In addition, men and women in the coed living situation tended to see each other more as equals, each sex capable of similar attainments and activities. We shared the same living conditions and participated in the same ways, holding office, cooking meals, cleaning, making policy decisions in the organizational structure of the cooperative. In this situation, women were not the "other," but

---

change the internal dynamic within the various Greek organizations as well as influence the relationship between men and women in our society. Thus "white feminism" is different from "African American feminism" and is discussed in a later chapter.
* I want to emphasize that my intent here is not to bash the Greek system. I am simply pointing out my observations as a former member.

both sexes were part of the "we." The thirteen or so houses that comprised the cooperative system in Ann Arbor were not racially diverse. I do not recall other African Americans who were affiliated with my particular house during the time period I was affiliated with it. In fact, I do not recall any other African Americans who lived in any of the thirteen houses at that time, although I am sure memory does not serve me well here.

It is intriguing to consider that at the fraternity there was also a heightened sense of heterosexuality. Trying to be with women was important, perhaps because it was so difficult. Alternative sexual orientations were never discussed. When they were, they often served to circumscribe the behavior of the members. To behave in ways that were not considered sanguine to the group were labeled as non-masculine on a continuum that led from heterosexuality to homosexuality. Again, it seems to me that this was a case where structure influenced social behavior and vice versa. Masculinity as defined in the fraternity supported less tolerance toward alternative sexual preferences.

In the Greek system there were informal traditions that served to locate boundaries between fraternities and sororities. Sorority members sometimes slipped into fraternity houses, and vice versa, to steal group pictures. In order to get them back, members had to go to the suspected Greek house and serenade the members in order to retrieve the pictures. The taking of pictures was always done by the opposite sex, thus a fraternity never would take the picture of another fraternity.

If I had to do it over again, I would have joined the fraternity next door to the one I joined. Back in the 1960s the Greek system lost popularity and some organizations went coed in order to survive. Some stayed coed well into the 70s. If there had been more coed Greek organizations when I was in college, it would have been much easier to join because the few that still existed would not have been seen as an oddity but part of the norm. But since the dominant form of Greek houses was same sex at that time, and I was young and easily swayed, it was not difficult to convince me that joining the mixed-sex fraternity was something very unusual perhaps even taboo. Issues of tainted masculinity, perhaps even related to homosexuality, were offered by some, not all, as reasons not to join a Greek organization that included women. "Real men don't do that." Today, the idea of living in such a communal situation with members of both sexes as sisters and brothers, part of a Greek situation, remains very appealing to me.

As of the writing of this chapter, an alleged incident of sexual assault involving members of the lacrosse team recently occurred at Duke University. Did the sex segregation of sports on college campuses play into what happened? Would such an incident, if it did happen, have occurred if the lacrosse team were sex integrated? Perhaps this is seen as a ludicrous idea. But I often ask classes why sports are not sex integrated. The response from students is usually one that indicates that men and women are physically different, and thus in sports like football, women usually don't have the "ability" to play. I then ask the class, why don't we change the rules so that both sexes can play? It is as if we have accepted that the rules of the game are dictated by nature.

It rarely occurs to my students that physical prowess may indeed differ between the sexes at this point in time, but in addition the rules of a particular sport could be changed to benefit and foster the inclusion of both sexes while taking into consideration the physical differences of each sex. If women are more flexible than men and men have more upper body brute strength, why not devise a game that takes both of these characteristics into consideration? Thus women could play certain positions and men could play other positions in the game. If women continue to be socialized to compete, it is unclear what women will be capable of accomplishing in comparison to men in the future. They are improving athletically more quickly than men.

The college campus as ivory tower

Although the college campus is often portrayed as an ivory tower or separate world, it may be more accurate to say that our nation's campuses are microcosms of the real world. When I first arrived on campus as an undergrad, I felt caught between two groups in a racially separated environment. My last three years of high school had provided me with access to African Americans. During that time I met my first girlfriend, who happened to be African American. But at college, I couldn't help but feel wedged between two distinct racial worlds in my dormitory of some 700 students. At meals there was segregation. African Americans and whites sat at separate tables. I felt much more comfortable sitting with whites from my hall because I knew them much more intimately. I also felt like a sell out when I did so. I didn't see stares or hear comments but I knew it was taking place. I had to learn to negotiate between the two worlds.

I was speaking with an older African American professor recently and she remarked how different college campuses seemed today compared to the time when I was in college in the mid 1970s. There is still immense social segregation on college campuses based on race, but the African American population seems to be somewhat different today than back then. As a student, when I walked across campus, every African American I passed nodded or even said hello. In turn I said hello to other African Americans as we passed each other during the course of the day. It was expected etiquette. Those that did not return a greeting were considered odd, even lost, or unable to cope with their racial identity, "trying to not be Black." Those seen as not willing to converse or interact with other African Americans were thought to be confused and it was thought that with time and patience they would eventually see and feel a sense of unity with other African Americans. There were many of us at Michigan at that time and while it was impossible to know the majority of African

Americans, there was a sense of open solidarity, recognition that no matter what our class background, how light our skin was, we were Black on an American college campus. The older professor I talked with indicated that African American students on college campuses today do not seem to have the same sense of open solidarity that they had a generation ago.

Many African American and white students still exist in segregated social environments on college campuses today, suggesting that institutions of higher learning do a poor job of creating new living situations on college campuses and that existing situations on college campuses may mimic a lifestyle and belief system held prior to attending college. Dickerson writes:

> Segregation on college campuses does occur. But it is not out of hostility but out of a sense of commonality.
>
> Self-segregation can occur as a means of support for marginilized groups...Likewise, "comfort level" can be an important factor in coping with pressures and feelings of detachment often felt by new college students. The latter mentioned type of support applies to all different race/ethnic groups, minority and majority. In no circumstances was self-segregation observed or self-reported to be practiced as a result of negative racial/ethnic outgroup sentiment...
>
> First, self-segregation should not be treated solely as a phenomenon occurring primarily among non-White groups. Nor should the practice be perceived as entirely negative. Secondly, support groups and cultural groups that celebrate different race/ethnic identities should be encouraged...
>
> As a sociological majority, whites are powerbrokers in society who have higher degrees of social mobility. With the greater ability to move within and about the social arrangements in society comes a responsibility to challenge oneself to cross race/ethnic boundaries that can cause negative forms of self-segregation.[85]

Both African Americans and Whites feel more comfortable with their own race. If one is part of the majority, recognizing characteristics associated with one's own group may not be as apparent as recognizing characteristics often associated with minority groups, that whites self segregate, too.

The evidence here seems to indicate that colleges and universities should push or enable students to be more uncomfortable during the college years by finding ways to foster the development of diverse social groups and networks. Thus there may be a fundamental tension between the financial bottom line of an institution of higher learning, the immediate retention of students and fostering contact between different groups on campus. Change needs to occur off campus as well in neighborhoods, occupations, and in the level of diversity in social networks, thereby fostering expectations among college students that diversity will continue in their lives after graduation.

The effects of environment on intimacy

It is true that the higher the class background marriages between African Americans and whites are more likely to occur. I do not believe that this should be construed to mean that individuals with increasing resources are more tolerant of difference. On the contrary, I tend to believe that the higher the class there actually may be more resistance to interracial marriage. What I do think happens is that the higher the class the more opportunity exists not necessarily to have repeated contact with someone of another race, but to act on those contacts and to have a romantic relationship should one decide to do so. Based on the overall literature on social characteristics of various class backgrounds, individuals in the lower classes may have fewer resources than those in higher classes and therefore may feel more likely to conform to the existing social characteristics, which are not to marry interracially, because they may feel more dependent on their family and communities for survival. But those in the higher classes, also subject to immense social pressure from family and friends, may also have more opportunity to strike out on their own because they have more resources, to leave their business and social acquaintances behind and to move to areas that are more accepting of "alternative" lifestyles. Thus greater resources afford individuals the chance to break with pressures to conform.

Because of overall differences between the two groups, interracial marriages play out differently between African Americans and whites than between other groups when the sex of each partner is considered. African American men are far more likely to marry white females than African American women who marry white males. When African American women do marry white males, the divorce rate is far higher as well because of different kinds of pressure these couples experience in their day-to-day living situations compared to the former.

Years ago I asked a white female in my class why she felt there were far more African American male/white female couples than white male/African American female couples. She believed that the overall position of each of the four groups below relative to the others may influence how group members are able or not able to feel a sense of commonality with each other during interracial social interaction. In terms of resources, when comparing the four groups, the following ranking from high to low exists:

(first)   white males
(second) African American males
(third)   white females
(fourth) African American females

In other words each of us, although we are individuals, is part of a group that often has similar experiences. If an African American woman who is married to or is dating a white male came home and told her husband, "honey, I really had a tough day and I think there is something happening to me on the job that is influenced by the fact I am a woman and African American," could he provide the same comfort to her as an African American male? I argue that probably *he could.*

If she continued to have different life experiences from his, is there a chance that these experiences would have a negative impact on the quality of their relationship? Divorce, between African American men and white females, is higher than it is for same-race couples[*] but not nearly as high as it is for African American women who are married to white males. There is something about African American female/white male marriages that does not allow these marriages as much longevity as African American male/white female marriages.

If African American women gain in overall group position in comparison to the other three groupings above, it is likely that the divorce rate will decrease for African American female/white male marriages (and African American women who are married to African American men) because the external pressures African American women experience will decrease. In other words, African American female/white male marriages would be expected to last longer when African American women as a group have more resources in our society, thus improving the overall position of this group relative to the other three groups: white males, African American males and white females.

More resources for African American women as a group should result in a lessening of stereotypes and prejudicial feelings toward and about African American women, a reduction in controlling images.[86] More power garnered by African American women might also result in more white males finding African American women more attractive not only because there would be a reduction of negative stereotypes as African American women as a group moved up the economic ladder, but African American women would be in a better position to affect changes in how African American women are perceived, namely through the media. Thus African American women as a group would be in a better position to control their own destiny.

---

[*] During a lengthy conversation I had with a white female student a number of years ago, who was dating an African American male, she described how stress outside of their relationship had influenced how they felt about each other. They were living together in a rural area that was almost all white. She was aware of the racism of many employers in that particular area. But yet, after a period of time, she started to question her boyfriend's manhood. She was able to get a job to pay for her share of the house they rented but he was not. Even though she was aware of why he was unable to get a job, there was still an adverse effect on their relationship. Not being able to pull his own weight to support payment of the rent adversely affected their relationship.

Your People?

In junior high school I was the spokesperson for the behavior of African Americans seen on the news. In a social studies class a teacher asked me to be the spokesperson for the "African American point of view." On another occasion, a friend had asked me why African Americans committed crimes. Their questions were not out of the norm during that time period. Reporters on television routinely asked African Americans, "How does the African American community feel about...?" Or, "now that King is dead, who will be the spokesperson for the African American community?" "How will African Americans feel about ...?" "What will be the reaction to...?"

It isn't that these questions were necessarily unsettling, but it is that they pointed to the existence of a great social distance between the two groups. I am reminded of the movie, *Roger and Me*, by Michael Moore. In one scene, Michael Moore goes to a yacht club seeking an interview with the chairperson of General Motors, Roger Smith. Moore asks the receptionist about Smith's whereabouts. The receptionist laughs incredulously at Moore's suggestion, "You want me to call Roger Smith?" This is a sociologically interesting moment in the film that is often overlooked. The idea that someone so low on the totem pole could call or even have the right to call someone at the very top is felt to be ludicrous by the receptionist. It just isn't accepted protocol.

In another scene, Moore goes to an athletic club seeking an interview with Smith. He is escorted to the door by a doorperson who is African American. Again the distance between the doorperson and Smith, the CEO of General Motors, is insurmountable. In fact the distance between the African American doorperson and the white receptionist who gives orders to the doorperson, seems equally as great.

The point is that the traditions of interaction within the confines of a given structure do not call for more contact between those on the bottom and those higher up so that they may understand each other better. New ways of operating within the confines of the structure, more involvement in the day-to-day operation of the organization at all levels of the company would produce a greater respect for those on the bottom and vice versa. Those on the bottom would have more power, more potential to influence policy and decision making, thus would be respected more, and perhaps would respect themselves more.*

I make the same comparison to the racialization of African Americans and whites in our society. A disproportionate number of African Americans, as a group, are on the bottom, have far less resources than whites, as a group. New ways of relating hierarchically to each other are needed. Finding ways to increase economic and social integration will produce not only more contact

---

* What is meant here is that those on the bottom would have more life choices.

between African Americans and whites but will go a long way toward reducing feelings of social distance while increasing feelings of commonality between African Americans and whites. Each group, African Americans and whites, with greater resource equality, would also be tempted to see each other as only Americans instead of as Americans who belong to a particular racial group.

Chapter Seven
Dating: African Americans and Whites

I arrived in Allegany County, Maryland a few months early during the summer so that I could find a house before I began teaching.[*] I vividly remember going to a state park along I-68 on an August evening with my wife and children to play on the playground and walk along the beach next to the lake. There were two other couples there, both interracial, and with their children. I was somewhat amazed to find so much diversity so quickly and I remember making a mental note to return to this playground as often as possible so that my children could benefit from being exposed to other kids like them. But on subsequent visits I never had that experience again. All of my children's playmates today are white.

During that initial visit to the park, I was unable to stop thinking about the two other couples there with us. I felt an urgency to ask them what it was like to live in Allegany County as an interracial family.[87] It was not hard to make small talk. But to push the conversation in the direction that would permit the parents to talk freely about issues related to race in that setting seemed a challenge.

Living in the South

For many of my students, Maryland is not "the South." But for me it is and moving there represented the beginning of a psychological reckoning. Living and working south of the Mason Dixon line for the first time in my life

---

[*] Portions of this chapter appeared in, *The Quality and Quantity of Contact: African Americans and Whites on College Campus*, edited by Robert M Moore III, published by University Press of America, Lanham, 2002.

beginning in 1998 gave me the opportunity to join various Southern sociology associations and to attend the annual conferences. I came face-to-face with some of the feelings I had harbored about this region since I was a young child often as a result of watching and listening to the news media. These events included sit-ins, beatings and murders.

One of the first conferences I attended after starting my new job was in Jackson, Mississippi. I called my father from the conference and told him where I was. There was absolute silence on the other end of the phone. He was a man about eighty years of age at that time. Half of his life had been lived prior to the civil rights struggles of the 1960s.[88]

This is a man who wasn't allowed to live in the freshman dorms at the university he attended in the 1940s because he was "Colored" even though physically he appeared white with very light skin like mine but with more wavy hair making it even more difficult to determine his race. When I told him I was in Jackson, this was not something he took lightly for a man of his generation. There was a momentary period of silence in our conversation.

In Jackson I asked the hotel van driver take me to see Medgar Evers' house. Evers was gunned down in his driveway on June 12th, 1963. He was a strong voice and active participant in the push to integrate institutions of higher education in Mississippi. He also fought to permit African Americans to use public accommodations and to allow participation in the political processes in the South. The van driver, an African American man in his 20s, took me there. Before departing the hotel he gave me a look and a smile as if to say, "those days were long ago and that life had changed greatly since the violent days of some forty years ago." On that trip to Jackson, I saw the supposed bullet holes still left in the outside walls of one of the dorms where a police officer allegedly shot at a man running through the historically African American campus of Jackson State University. This was many years ago when there was much unrest on the nation's university and college campuses. I also had the opportunity to talk with an individual affiliated with the mayor's cabinet, a white female. She told me she had been married to an African American man, who had died of natural causes a few years earlier. I found this to be, in my mind, very unique and I felt compelled to ask what sort of problems she had experienced. She didn't outright deny that there had been problems, although it felt like she was close to doing so, but she said with great conviction and feelings similar to those conveyed by the van driver, that Mississippi had changed.

The state where Emmet Till, the fourteen year old African American boy visiting from the North for the summer, who spoke to a white female on a dare from his friends and then was murdered for doing so some 40 years ago, had changed! I was amazed. During that brief trip to Jackson I visited various museums and was vividly reminded of Mississippi's past. But I also learned that Mississippi had pushed forward.

How much change has there been?

How much change has there really been in America? Although there seems to be plenty of publicity about interracial marriages, as a total percent of all marriages, the number for black/white marriages is still very small, about one half of one percent.

African American/White Married Couples and All Married Couples in the United States, 1992.

Type	Totals
All married couples	53,512,000
Black/White married couples	246,000

Source: U.S. Bureau of the Census. Table 1. Race of Wife by Race of Husband

Given that our nation's campuses have been traditionally viewed as walled off from society, thus the idea of an ivory tower, one would intuitively think that social forces from the outside would be negligible in determining or producing patterns of interracial dating on campus (Newcomb et al, 1967). Interracial dating among students should therefore happen freely and randomly. As many African American females as African American males should date white males and females, respectively.

Crossing Over, Friendship before Romance

About ten years ago I conducted an exploratory study of dating between African Americans and whites at a small private liberal arts university located in a rural setting in a mid-Atlantic state. Based on conversations I have had with students today, I have no reason to suspect there has been much change in the social behavior of students compared to the time period when I conducted the study. I was only interested in studying serious relationships between members of each "race." I defined serious for the purpose of the research as having dated for four or more months.

I found that more than half of the African American males at River University[*] had dated interracially at the time of the study, some before

---

[*] River University is a fictitious name for the university.

attending college and others for the first time while in college. The university where the study was conducted had a student body of only about twelve hundred. It was rather costly to attend. A significant portion of the student body was from outside the state.[89] The following conclusions were drawn:

1. Very few interracial relationships had developed as a result of love at first sight. Relationships usually involved frequent but often incidental contact.

2. African American men did not feel completely at ease when talking to white females.

3. African American women felt very distant from white males and did not trust their motives although they expressed an openness to marry a white male should one be found that was culturally compatible.

4. *Myth making* occurred to explain why interracial dating happened. Myth making, stereotypical reasons given for dating, served to keep racial boundaries in tact.

5. White females who were active members of predominantly white organizations on campus did not date interracially as often as white females who did not join these organizations.

6. Whites who dated interracially reported new ways of *seeing* the world as a result of interracial dating.

7. An increase in the size of African Americans on a college campus would probably bring a lower percentage of interracial dating.

8. The college experience fostered more African American males to date white females than the number of African American females who dated white males while in college.

How interracial relationships develop

I found that love at first site did not play a role in the initial contacts that eventually led to two people of different racial backgrounds dating. It was repeated chance encounters rather than "chasing" that eventually led to interracial dating. Although this defies some stereotypes, for example, African American males as aggressive and who lust after white females, or African American women as promiscuous, it also possibly points to the conclusion that those who interracially date do not jump into these relationships haphazardly.

Dormitories, cafeterias and the library were common places for an initial series of contacts. For example, Jack (African American) saw a woman (white) in the lobby of the library wearing a jacket with the insignia of a high school that was in his hometown. He asked her if she knew some of his friends who had attended that particular high school. It turned out that she did and in fact had attended that high school. They shared rides home out of convenience during school breaks. During the rides they became friends and eventually began dating. Although she was younger than Jack, they continued to date after he graduated. He went to graduate school and she transferred to an undergraduate institution near his graduate school to be with him.

In another situation, both students, African American male and white female, after they had finished practice with their respective athletic teams, ate meals in a nearly empty cafeteria. Rather than eat alone they began to eat with each other. They became friends first and then dated. Another couple met through a roommate because he (African American male) had befriended the roommate (white) and thus repeated incidental contact led to dating the roommate. In another situation, the individuals met because they lived in the same dormitory and often sat in the same common area. They used to meet in a lounge after dates with other people of the same race and tell each other how bad their evenings had been. A semester went by before they finally decided that perhaps they should try dating each other.

For some, love at first sight may explain why some people date, but it was certainly not the case for interracial couples at River University. Frequent contact by chance was a better explanation and feelings that each person had something in common with the other.[90]

Tales of Caution: Evidence of a Racial Divide

There was other evidence of possible barriers related to race. Some African American men expressed caution when casually interacting with white females:

> Jack - I couldn't take as many chances as my white male friends. I made very sure about the signals I received. I knew the consequences could possibly be much greater for an African American male than for a white male if my behavior was perceived as being aggressive or forward.[91]

The consequences Jack, a senior, spoke of were related to the possibility of being falsely accused of harassment or even worse sexual assault. Jack had been called as a witness in a student judiciary inquiry in an alleged attempted rape by one of his white fraternity brothers (predominantly white fraternity). He vividly remembered the hearing even though several years had passed. He felt sure that if the alleged perpetrator had been an African American male the call for judgement would have been swift, harsher and handled by the local police instead of university staff. I believe all matters of sexual assault should be handled by the police. But the point is that Jack felt there was a dual system, one for whites and the other for African Americans.

Although written over fifty years ago, Merton expressed similar ideas about social distance between African Americans and whites:

> ... the contacts between members of different racial castes are regulated by codes of racial etiquette so that there are few opportunities for relationships not involving considerable social distance. [92]

Incidental contact and friendship were usually a precursor to actual dating. African American men expressed awareness of the negative stereotypes that existed in society and how it affected their own behavior on campus[93]. Not all white females were willing to let friendship develop into a relationship (see below). Interracial relationships were thus not randomly distributed throughout the student body.

African American Women and White Males

Issues related to race are made more complex when gender is considered. When asked to rank who was more willing to date or marry interracially, African American women were felt to be the least likely by all participants in the study. White males were ranked next to last, white females second from the top, and African American men at the top. Although the majority of African American women did feel a greater social distance than that felt by African American males to white females, many African American women expressed openness to the idea of dating a white male if they could find someone who they felt culturally close to and someone they could trust. Thus, they did not rule out the idea but attached conditions.

At the same time, the majority of African American women felt that white males were too culturally distant from them:

> **Barbara** (African American)– I don't always want to be constantly teaching someone. My mother always said you want to date someone from the same background as you. I never understood that. Now I do.

> **Keisha** (African American) – I think we [as] Black women are more mature [than] white men. [They] can't relate to our needs and values, some of them not at all. When we observe white men...they see things that are totally different.

African American women perceived white males to be more interested in being able to tell others they had had sex with an African American woman than in having a relationship thus there was the issue of trust:

Tara (African American) – I know a lot of white guys if they see an attractive Black female probably would like to say I slept with a Black girl.

Although there was a perception that African American males were more willing than African American females to date interracially, and indeed most African American males had had a serious interracial relationship by the end of their senior year at River, I found that more African American males were initially (when they arrived at River) absolutely opposed to interracial dating than African American females when asked to think back about how they felt when they first arrived on campus. William (African American) was a transfer student who played basketball for River. He was initially against interracial dating. At his previous university, one day he visited his best friend (African American). His friend called for the woman upstairs to come down so he could introduce her to William. His friend's new girlfriend was white. William was shocked and silently angry. He couldn't believe his friend was dating interracially. Feeling betrayed he did not talk to his best friend for over a year.

After William transferred to River, his feelings about interracial dating began to slowly change, he told me, given time and repeated exposure to other African American men who were dating white females. At the time of the interview with him he was in a relationship with a white female from the surrounding community. The areas that surrounded River were almost entirely white, with probably less than one percent of the entire county African American.

As a group, African Americans had had far more contact with whites prior to college than whites had had with African Americans. African American men and even African American women were more likely to have dated interracially prior to college compared to white students. But at River it was African American men who were more likely to have dated interracially than African American women by the end of their senior year.

Unlike African American females, interracial dating prior to college for African American men did not predict whether they would date interracially while in college. But dating experiences for African American women prior to college did predict if they would date interracially while in college. If an African American woman had not dated interracially while in high school she was very unlikely to do so in college. If she did date interracially before college she was likely to continue to do so. This may speak profoundly to the different social situations available that may potentially enrich college social experiences for African American men and women and perhaps to all men and women on college campuses.

Colleges, often seen and felt as middle class enclaves with accompanying middle class values, based on River, seem to enable more African American men than women to *cross over* and date interracially. If there is a correlation between social behavior and access to various class strata, college campuses, by enabling more African American men to date interracially than African American females, may be reproducing the current hierarchical structure found today, from highest to lowest in terms of wealth, income and power: white males, African American males, white females, and last, African American females.

I didn't set out to date a black man!

I found very few white females (or others) in my study of serious long term (4 or more months) interracial relationships to have a predisposition to date African American men. Only one expressed a feeling that she specifically liked dating interracially. In fact many women came from neighborhoods where friends and family were openly opposed to it.

Bobbie, white, explained how her grandfather refused to talk to her after learning the racial identity of her boyfriend. Her parents cut her off financially. Amanda, white, spoke of the extreme negative and open hostility people in her rural town expressed when they saw a person of color.[94] Students who dated interracially at River did not do so for reasons of social experimentation. Their relationships developed because of propinquity, incidental contact.

Almost every white female who had dated or was dating interracially told a story about an incident at a party on campus where a white male, usually after drinking, would comment: "so you are down with the brown," or "what's wrong, a white man isn't good enough for you?" But almost all of the students who interracially dated felt strongly that the campus atmosphere was quite tolerant regardless of these comments.

White females who dated interracially were not rebelling against their parents and most had loving relationships and good communication with their parents. Only one of the women considered race to be a variable that attracted her to her partner. It is hard to make a case that rebellion or a predisposition to date interracially based on cultural or physical attraction to African American men was relevant in explaining why white females dated interracially. While in college almost all considered dating white males and most had. Kouri and Lasswell found no evidence of rebellion as a determinant of interracial marriage in their study of Los Angeles married couples.[95]

Why do some people and situations stand out?

Although a good portion of my students in my classes state that they would marry someone of another race, there are still some who say that interracial marriage is not for them. The reasons sometimes vary according to each group. When African American students reject interracial marriage it is usually based on feelings of social distance from whites. African American students often cite feelings of cultural difference. Those who identify as white who indicate that interracial marriage is not for them also cite feelings of cultural difference, but some express concern that a child who has one African American and one white parent may have troubling fitting in. I have never heard someone who identifies as African American express a similar concern. My sense is that what many African Americans feel and routinely experience is felt to be similar to what they would imagine interracial children would experience.[96]

I think what it means to be normal to not think about who I am racially. There would be a sense of invisibility. On the other hand this is not possible because there is still need to recognize that African Americans experience a disproportionate level of social problems. As long as inequity exists, it will be quite hard to feel invisible for a variety of reasons. One, there is need to recognize that African Americans are disproportionately affected by particular social problems in order to find solutions, to keep awareness high. Two, social problems that affect African Americans are likely to generate negative stereotypes thereby fostering discriminatory behavior against African Americans.

I remember coming home from elementary school one day and telling my father I just didn't feel like I fit in. He immediately told me, "You are exposed." I knew exactly what he meant, but I didn't want to believe it was true. I wanted to fit in and be like my classmates. I pushed his thoughts aside. Indeed, I had a tendency to push aside black history books at that time as well. I didn't want to be different from my classmates, at least not in a way that seemed to draw negativity my direction.

Given that our society is still quite segregated, people and situations that are not common to our everyday perusal still stand out, strike an awkward dissonant chord, and cause us to do a double take. Although I have traveled back and forth through Vermont and New Hampshire on the way to Maine to visit my wife's family, I still think about race in some way on these visits. It is unavoidable to me. Compared to many other states, very few African Americans live there. I have spent many days in these areas without seeing someone who was African American.

In America, even though I may be in areas with very few African Americans, I recognize that I am still part of the same social system thus subject to the same media. Fewer African Americans does not mean I stop questioning issues related to race. I routinely ask myself why there is so little diversity in these states and simple answers based on African Americans not wanting to live in such rural and remote places do not cut it.

Merging of in-group and out-group within the Individual

In my study of interracial dating on college campuses it became evident that one of the important side effects of dating interracially was that white females, as well as white males that dated interracially, became more sensitive to issues related to race. Dawn, a white female, became more aware of intolerance when expressed in social situations. Only two white males who had dated interracially were located and took part in the study. They became more sensitive to issues related to race as well.

Robert, a white male who was an alumnus, said he was much more conscious of race as a result of dating an African American woman, still a student at the university. They were engaged to be married at the time of the interview. He talked about walking into various offices while traveling on business and seeing managerial levels all with white employees and lower levels predominantly staffed by minorities. He said he had never noticed race before dating interracially.

Whites who dated interracially also became aware of unusual behavior exhibited by strangers such as stares they received when off campus while in stores. One couple amusingly indicated that they purposively showed more affection with each other in local stores when they became aware of someone looking at them in what they perceived to be a disapproving manner.

It is common in the literature to read about African Americans when alone or with other African Americans who feel a gaze or a sense of being treated differently.[97] To receive stares when interracially dating was not a new experience for African Americans but it was for whites. This suggested that African Americans and whites often have different life experiences.

Jane Elliot, famous for her films showing people in workshops divided on the basis of eye color, argues that people of color are forced to know what it means to live in a "white world" for purposes of survival but the opposite is rarely the case. In a very real sense, whites who dated interracially became very aware that they were more than just an individual but that they were in fact a white person. Being aware that one was experiencing something different did not stop these things from happening.

My interviews with students at River uncovered situational contexts that profoundly altered the way white students who had or were interracially dating think about race and what race meant in the overall structure of our society.[98] Students became more aware of how much of a factor race really was in our society.[99]

Acculturation is usually thought of as occurring when a minority group adopts the culture of the majority society. In this case white females and white males that interracially dated adopted ways of seeing and experiencing society from the perspective of someone who experiences *difference* on a routine basis, a person of color. For African Americans who dated interracially this had already occurred – part of the socialization process while growing up. Thus there was no noted change for African Americans in the amount of awareness they felt in regard to issues and situations related to race.

Keeping the Fence Up

I found that rumors and stereotypes abounded at River University to explain why interracial dating occurred. When asked about interracial dating, the majority of African American women believed African American men were using white females for a variety of reasons including for sex, to do laundry, or to obtain access to a nice car and more. When asked how they came to have these feelings, many responded that African American men had told them so. But in reality, this was not the case.

African American men who refused to date white females voiced similar feelings about African American men who did. The findings indicated that the propagation of these ideas served to maintain a feeling of solidarity or community among African American students. These feelings, *myth making*, served to mask the true nature of interracial dating between African American males and white females. Interracial-dating partners really did care about each other and these myths served to perhaps sustain a positive self-identity.[100] These myths served to reduce role inconsistency, the expectation that existed that because one was African American one was supposed to behave in certain ways. The myths explained, falsely, why behavior that was beyond role expectations associated with membership in a particular race had occurred.

Gordon wrote about "marginal people" or people who straddle two groups.[101] He discussed assimilation[102] as a process whereby people take on "memories, sentiments, and attitudes of other persons or groups, and by sharing their experience and history, are incorporated with them in a common cultural life." The results of my interviews suggested that whites that date interracially are able to have a deeper understanding of race relations in America.

African American men made a distinction between dating and "casual" sex whereas African American women saw dating and sex more intricately intertwined. William, when he was opposed to interracial dating, was not opposed to having sex with a white female. He made a clear distinction between having sex and dating. These findings echo those by other researchers on differences between men and women concerning sex and love regardless of race.[103] Although some African American men and women chose not to date interracially, most did not object to those who did. Their objections were limited to their own lifestyles and thus they felt what other people of color did was their own business.

Maintaining Whiteness

One third of all female students at River at the time of the study were in a sorority. Most of the white females who dated interracially were not. A common feeling was that joining a sorority was akin to buying friends.

> **Samantha** (white) - I don't know why you need a sorority to be a name [on campus].

> **Joanna** (white) - No desire not at all to join a sorority. I think it is kind of retarded and I don't have the money – not worth buying your friends.

It is likely that white females who dated interracially were more socially independent than many who did not. The implications here are that membership in groups that lack diversity may inhibit certain types of social behavior, particularly interracial dating.

Similar to all-male groups that may inadvertently reinforce masculinity, predominantly white organizations may inadvertently promote characteristics associated with being white, such as standards of beauty, simply because alternative ideas and characteristics are less available. Also, non-integrated residential areas, occupations and social networks in everyday real life off campus may also serve to inhibit more positive feelings between African Americans and whites.

Social Capital and Inter-race Contact: part of myth making

African American women also thought that many African American men on campus were popular.

> **Janice** (African American) – Just here at school most Black males are football players and they look really good. African American males who don't play sports tend to socialize with African American females and they don't tend to have white females swooning over them.

Many did not seek out or join formal social groups. Economic variables emphasizing the class background of students – since most sororities and fraternities ask members to pay dues – did not explain why these women did not join a sorority. According to Gavazzi, people from rural areas are more independent than people from suburban backgrounds.[104] It is possible that some people who join sororities do so to reduce feelings of social alienation. Sororities do reduce social alienation significantly.[105] Being more independent there may be less of a need to join. This would suggest that organizations that tend not to be very diverse, such as sororities, also inhibit white females from dating interracially.[106]

There is also tremendous conformity of behavior. Incidence of heavy drinking increases in sororities after joining.[107] Eating disorders, desire for a more thin body, issues related to appearance and higher dissatisfaction with ones body in general are far more prevalent in white sororities than among non-sorority members or African American sororities.[108] Again, this suggests that members in a white sorority have a higher tendency to try and imitate the values, norms and trends evident in society at-large more so than women who do not join Greek organizations. It should also be noted that Greek members are more concerned about what their peers will think about their behavior and are less likely to date interracially than non-Greek members.[109]

I found that more white females who dated interracially were from rural backgrounds. It isn't clear why more rural white males did not show up in the study. It is possible that rural white males are more similar to suburban white males than white rural females to white suburban females. Men as a group tend to show higher feelings of social alienation than women.[110]

It also may be true that many rural women had not been exposed to stereotypes and thus when an opportunity to date came about, and the person happened to be of another race, they were more likely to proceed with dating than someone from a suburban background[111]. These findings suggest, and indeed the study was exploratory so more work is needed, that whites who interracially date perceive the world differently before the relationship begins than whites who do not interracially date. The small number of interracial marriages in America may suggests a uniformity of behavior among whites, even though post industrial societies are more fast paced than industrial ones, that may inhibit a majority of whites from forming long-term relationships with African Americans.

Sex Ratio

An increase in the number of African American students as well as an increase in the number relative to the overall size of the student body would probably decrease the percentage of interracially - dating couples[112]. Research by Monahan in upstate New York on interracially - married couples reached a similar conclusion. As the number of non-whites in an area increased, the number of interracial marriages actually decreased[113]. Only two percent of the student body at River was African American.

Studies by sociologists suggest that when there are relatively few African Americans in a given area in proportion to the white population, African Americans have more contact with whites.[114] It may also suggest that whites may feel more threatened in some ways when the number of African Americans reaches a certain level.[115]

In white residential neighborhoods this is often referred to as a "tipping point," the percentage of African Americans that when reached will begin to drive whites from the neighborhood. The continued pushing out from urban America by African Americans into the inner rings of the suburbs may have produced an overall sense among many whites in America that a suburban tipping point may have occurred or is close and thus there are a massive number of whites who are now moving away from metropolitan areas altogether.[116]

These ideas may lead to intriguing future hypotheses about "race ratios" or trying to quantify a "critical mass" theory in regard to race relations in a given area. African American men in my study at River expressed feelings of having little choice but to date white females. An increase in the number of African American students would allow African American men and women to have more choices of potential dating partners who are African American. This may increase social pressure against interracial dating.

Contrary to the stereotypes some may hold, African American men did not favor dating white females over African American females. Jonathan, an African American male, thought dating an African American female on campus to be "like dating someone in your family." Although there were slightly more African American women than men on campus, very few dating relationships had developed between African American men and women. Again, since African Americans made up approximately two percent of the student body, there may have been too few to provide choices for dating partners intra-racially. If there were more African Americans at River, some African American men may have felt more pressure to date within "their" race.

African American men expressed a willingness to date African American women and almost all had done so before college. Many more African American women than African American men said they were either not dating at all or were dating someone off campus, "back home." Almost all African American men and women interviewed expressed pride in being African American with one exception. Don, for example, believed white females to be more "refined" and "cultured" than African American women. He didn't identify with being African American but with the West Indian roots of his parents. Perhaps this was a factor in his beliefs. He was an exception.

Consider the Whole Picture

At the same time as students seem to express a heightened sense of individualism, the idea that we are all so unique that it borders on some sort of biological or genetic origin, students still feel a deep sense of being raced. What is more interesting is that although students believe there are racial differences, they are unable to entertain a connection to a sense of being raced to the larger social system. Internalization of individualism is so strong that large collective entities, a sense of race, are taken for granted, just another part of individualism. As mentioned in an earlier chapter, even to have a dating or marriage preference that excludes an entire race is seen as okay, just another preference, like wearing an orange versus a gray shirt today, "as long as it does not affect me personally."

Different life experiences

African American women may not be as included in the mainstream social life of River University as African American men. The "social distance" felt between African American women and white males was greater than that between African American men and white females. These findings further suggest that, especially in regard to a feminist perspective, African American females and white females have different life experiences and that it may be appropriate to consider what Boca Zinn calls a "multiracial feminist" perspective.[117] But the findings also suggest that whites become much more sensitive to issues of race as a result having dated interracially. American standards of beauty may also influence white males to seek only white females.

The existence of so many interracial relationships on a small college campus, although predominantly African American male-white female, can be viewed as a good reason to believe "race relations" were good at the university and probably much better than a generation ago. The patterns found on campus seem to echo what occurred off campus. There was some dating between white males and African American females but certainly not to the extent of that between African American males and white females.

It may be that African American females and white males are not integrated in the life of the college in ways that allowed for intimate relations to develop between them. Even so the college experience at River affected African American men in a different way than it did African American women.

Many River Universities exist and it is safe to conclude that similar social behavior occurs - interracial dating occurs and couples feel comfortable on campus to do so. Partners at River felt a sense of commonality with each other that deepened as the relationship progressed and affected how one perceived one's "racial identity" or "racial space."

Merton proposed, over fifty years ago, that there were greater incentives for the formation of African American male-white female couples than vice versa. He hypothesized that African American males by marrying white females gained social status by marrying someone who is white. White females could gain economic status because, according to Davis and Merton, white females were more likely to marry "up".[118] Thus it was a mutual trade so to speak. The same could not be said for white males marrying African American females. One could not speak of a mutual trade.

Others have refuted Davis and Merton's theories.[119] Those who date interracially at River expressed feelings of shared similarities as a primary reason for dating each other. African American males did not show any indications that dating interracially was motivated by wanting to increase social status on campus. White females, nor others who dated interracially, did not give any indication that they dated interracially as a way of improving their economic status.

It is true that American men regardless of race are more prone than American women to initially value physical attraction in perspective dating partners.[120] Evidence also points out that women today have moved closer to male sexual practices compared to women a generation ago, suggesting that socialization does play an important part in influencing not only individual but group behavior.

The evidence in my exploratory study of River suggested that contrary to popular opinion, physical attraction is less important as a mechanism that promotes the formation of interracial couples than it may be for same-race couples. The evidence presented also shows that white students who interracially date change the way they see the world. It is the opinion of this writer that social behavior on our nation's college campuses very much reflects the overall inequality between African Americans and whites off campus.

Chapter Eight
Race and women

I have considered myself a feminist for at least a couple decades, since before I entered graduate school. In fact I have been one of the few, if not only man, involved in various groups concerned about the quality of life for women on campus, at both universities where I have taught. I have also been, at one time or another, the only African American, not from another country, with tenure at each institution where I have taught full time. It is still my belief that the fate of women and African Americans is connected. If discrimination rises for one I believe it is likely to rise for the other.

My feminism pushes the idea that men can lead more positive and enriching lives by practicing values that are traditionally and perhaps stereotypically associated with women such as nurturance, more emotional, sharing, less competitive and more. I would like to see a continued blurring of gender roles, less emphasis on a division between femininity and masculinity. For this to be achieved I believe it is important that resources be available in our society to support individuals and families lead better lives such as inexpensive but quality daycare, development of a sense of community in neighborhoods, more involvement of parents and other adults in the lives of children and young adults.

I have had the privilege to facilitate over forty students engaged in an Independent Study, a one-on-one course with a professor. The topics we have covered have varied but most have dealt with issues related to race. Recently, I worked with two white females, each on a different occasion, who wanted to find out more about Black feminism. Both became interested as a result of long discussions with me during a previous semester while enrolled in one of my regular classes. One is now a graduate student in a Women's Studies program at a large Midwestern university.

My relationship with the two students could be characterized as intellectually contentiousness but quite positive, a situation I believe that initially encouraged both to do an Independent Study with me. I continually advanced the position that white feminism and black feminism were different.[121] Both women found my position difficult to accept since I seemed to be advocating a separation between women based on race and therefore diminishing the potential of women to change society since they would be divided rather than united.

My students tended to be much more individualistic than me, pushing equality in the workplace whereas I pushed access to opportunity; a more systemic approach that implied not all women operated on the same playing field or could get their foot in the door. I didn't disagree with their ideas but simply expanded on them to include possible ways all women could have access to a similar quality of life especially poor women. A major difference between the two feminisms I suggested was that black feminism was concerned about black men whereas white feminism was not.

African American and white females often have divergent opinions and expectations about how to balance family and work after graduation from college. African American women in my classroom are more likely to expect to work continuously rather than take time off to care for a new born. I have heard very few African American women in my classrooms claim that they would like to be a "soccer mom" after college. It does not mean the desire is not there, but this idea is rarely articulated.

> When asked, "Do you recall your father or mother stressing that you should have an occupation to succeed in life?" racial differences appear. Ninety-four percent of all Black respondents [women] said yes. ...In contrast, only 70 percent of the white middle class and 56 percent of the white working-class women indicated that their parents stressed that an occupation was needed for success.[122]

> We asked, "Do your recall your mother or father emphasizing that marriage should be your primary life goal?"...Virtually no Black parents stressed marriage as the primary life goal (6 percent of the working class and 4 percent of the middle class), but significantly more white parents did (22 percent of the working class and 18 percent of the middle class).[123]

On the other hand, there is usually a small number of white female students in my classes who openly proclaim their desire to be at home with their children after they are born, at least for a specified period of time.

White heterosexual females have a greater availability of men from whom to choose as well. Their social networks are often more socially diverse, i.e., many more white males to choose, but not more racially diverse, according to Patricia Hill Collins.[124] African American heterosexual women have a tougher time (due to the lack of available men) finding a husband than their white counterparts. The ratio of available African American men to available African American woman is smaller than the number of white males to white females.[125] It is no wonder that fewer African American women openly express a desire to be a soccer mom.

In fact I hear very little discussion by African American women about marriage. This does not mean the desire is not present, it simply is not articulated as loudly. Given the social distance felt between African American women and white males, plus there is still a separation of the two groups socially, for instance on college campuses, dating and marrying white males does not seem to be an option at this point.

Should more African American men become available in the future, there is every reason to believe that the ideas expressed by white females about marriage, family and the raising of children will be expressed more openly by African Americans as well. In the meantime, feelings of cultural difference between African Americans and whites, i.e., the image of a strong matriarchal black woman compared to a less strong white female, mislead us. For in fact, it isn't necessarily cultural differences that lead to social behavior, it is also the effects of inequality that lead us to believe in this case that there are cultural differences; African American men face much more discrimination than white males and therefore African American women are raised to be more independent than white females.

Therefore white and black feminism diverge on the issue of what equality means. African American feminists push for ways to help African American men that may include a more systemic analysis of why African American men are in the position they are today. Such analyses take into consideration the penal system, the need to build viable communities where men can be included in family life and be role models to children and young adults, and issues related to work, thus how people who are on the bottom can sustain themselves.

The everyday stresses that so many African American women feel because of their disproportionate exposure to different life experiences has produced an outlook on life that is different from that of many white females. It doesn't mean African American and white females do not have the same goals, but that their expectations of achieving those goals may be different. Although most white females today are no longer socialized to believe that college is a place to find a husband, more compared to African American females are able to find love at their respective institutions of higher learning.[126] Since many white females today are told by their mothers to be prepared for divorce, thus are pushed to obtain the necessary credentials to be able to survive on their own, African

American women are not as likely to be so optimistic about connecting romance and work after college.

White feminists are more vocal in their support of strategies that mix working and raising a family such as onsite daycare and paternal leave policies. African American feminists go one step further and tend to be more politically left of white feminists because they have more need to look at why African American men are in trouble with the law in such large numbers, are being murdered and are unable to complete school, as well as other social problems that affect African American men. The breath of issues for African American feminists is broader, perhaps too broad for many white feminists.

Many African American women, because so many African American men have been unable to contribute financially to the formation and maintenance of a family because of racism, have had a different outlook than many white females about gender roles and family:

> ...housework has never been the central focus of Black women's lives. They have largely escaped the psychological damage industrial capitalism inflicted on white middle-class housewives, whose alleged virtues were feminine weakness and wifely submissiveness.[127]

They were never expected to conform or react in an expected or desired way as white females were.

I believe that during the early days of mainstream feminism in the 1960s, white feminists may have had different goals than many white feminists today espouse. Values traditionally associated with being a woman such as being more communal or placing emphasis on the group, being able to be emotional and nurturing and sharing were to be embraced. As we have moved deeper into post industrialization, mainstream feminism seems to have incorporated more of a male model such as a greater emphasis on the individual, less concern about the emotional well being of employees in the workplace and being more competitive. Thus mainstream feminist movements today tend to embrace traditional male characteristics rather than those that were considered traditionally more associated with women.

Mainstream feminism today seems to encourage women to play by the same rules of the game as men, thus the existing rules, rather than to change the rules.*

---

* I often tell my students that I am an old-school feminist, based on what I know of the early 60s, when traditional values associated with femininity such as an emphasis on the group, communality, the sharing of emotions and nurturance were more associated with feminism than they are today. I tell my students that it is "we" men who commit the most crime, more violent in general and that we could lead better lives if we accepted and lived by the values stereotypically associated with femininity. Many of my students today, especially women, reject association with those "traditional" values and see them as a

This tends to exclude people of color. Dill points out the historical origins of difference between African American women and white women.

> Unlike white women, racial-ethnic women experienced the oppressions of a patriarchal society but were denied the protections and buffering of a patriarchal family. Their families suffered as a direct result of the organization of the labor systems in which they participated.[128]

The lower the class the more divorce there is. African Americans have a higher rate of family break up and single parenthood not because there is less inclination to form families or because of cultural values and norms passed down from generation to generation, but because contemporary financial circumstances make it tougher to form families and to keep families together once they are formed.

Why are there more African American male/white female couples?

The possibility that African American men and white females may see the world more similarly, compared to African American women and white males, thus there are far more interracial relationships between African American males and white females than the ladder, is quite provocative.

> The combined forces of racism and sexism often make the black female graduate experience differ in kind from that of the black male experience. While he may be subjected to racial biases, his maleness may serve to mediate the extent to which he will be attacked, dominated, etc.[129]

African American women may feel a greater sense of bonding with each other and thus place less emphasis on individualism.

> When we asked the white women in the study the following question: "Generally, do you feel you owe a lot for the help given to you by your family and relatives?" many were perplexed and asked what the question meant. In contrast, both the working- and middle-class Black women tended to respond immediately that they felt a sense of obligation to family and friends in return for the support they had received.[130]

> The mainstream model of community stresses the rights of individuals to make decisions in their own self-interest, regardless of the impact on the larger society.[131] This model may explain relations to community or origin

---

hindrance if not examples of sexism when espoused by men, instead of a once "revolutionary" ideology that could have enabled men to be better people.

for mobile white males but cannot be generalized to other racial and gender groups.[132]

African American men on college campuses may move closer to the patriarchal values associated with white masculinity than African American women move or are able to move toward the values associated with white femininity. Issues of gender and class collide in ways that complicate already existing racial boundaries.

If I had to define my own feminism, it represents a mixture of what I perceived to be old-school mainstream feminism, that placed emphasis on traditional values of sharing, nurturance and the expression of emotions, and what I believe Black feminism is today, which is to provide more access to resources for African Americans, all Americans, so that a better quality of life can be possible, families can be formed and maintained, and communities can be viable places to live.

Conclusion
Coming to Grips with Race in America

I do think my life would have been easier if I had married an African American woman, though not necessarily happier. Race is still strongly felt by so many in our society. There probably would not be as many quick glances by strangers if I were in a same-race relationship. I would attract less attention. I often have a feeling of being in the limelight as if I am performing. I desire to be able to step off the stage for a rest.

Given the situational contexts I was exposed to when I was raised, an all white neighborhood and schools during a period when an emphasis was placed on assimilation and not multiculturalism, and given that my skin is fair, it is not surprising that some would have assumed that I would marry or even had a preference for a white female. I did learn to see and feel life, including standards of beauty, political outlooks, and more, from both sides of the color line. But I always knew who I was, African American.

The book that has moved me the most to think deeply about race and identity is James Weldon Johnson's, *Auto-Biography of an Ex-Colored Man*, published almost 100 years ago. The following quote from the book described a situation when the protagonist, a very fair African American male passing for white and living in Europe with his American wife, who is white, is about to reveal his secret to her, that he is really African American.

> Up to this time I had assumed and played my role as a white man with a certain degree of nonchalance, a carelessness as to the outcome, which made the whole thing more amusing to me than serious; but now I ceased to regard "being a white man" as a sort of practical joke. My acting had called for mere external effects. Now I began to doubt my ability to play the part. I watched her to see if she were scrutinizing me, to see if she was looking for anything in me which made me differ from the other men she knew...

...--Duty; and bending over her hand in mine, I said; "Yes, I love you; but there is something more, too, that I must tell you." Then I felt her hand grow cold, and when I looked up, she was gazing at me with a wild, fixed stare as though I was some object she had never seen...[133]

There were times in my childhood when I was somewhat reticent to speak, when there was a discussion about race. Still today I feel a constant weight in certain situations, as if I harbor a secret that lurks inside of me that is bound to leak out. I know I am Black. "They" know I am Black. But to be "Black" comes with a price to be paid, to be seen and treated differently. Thus there is sometimes a desire to keep something hidden. I must be sure that people do not see the "real" me and thereby link me with the negative stereotypes so pervasive in our society that derogatorily label and box African Americans.

Johnson's book, written in the early 20th century, strikes a cord even today. To be or act white may mean to be on constant guard that one is not associated with the "bad elements." It is to behave in a manner that does not invite an unnecessary negative reaction: being conscious of what it means to others to be African American when browsing in a store, talking in ways to law enforcement personnel that will not trigger adverse reactions, contributing to a classroom discussion in ways that do not produce labels from classmates that one is loud or angry, hiding disappointment and being on guard when talking to white females so as not to give the wrong impression as to one's motives. To be African American is to be aware of how to negotiate both sides of the color line.

Resource Equity Model

I routinely assign Stephen Steinberg's (1989) book, *The Ethnic Myth,* in my class on race. The implication is that when two groups have reached a state of resource equality relative to the other, the boundaries between the two groups begin to fade and may even wither completely. Steinberg's book is about Eastern and Southern Europeans who are able, many started their economic climb in America by working in factories, to enter the burgeoning middle class after World War II.[134]

African Americans may indeed one day have resource equality relative to whites. But, this does not mean there will be a synthesis of identity between the two groups. The wrongs of the past may be too deep and entrenched in all Americans to be overcome. We will therefore need to remain vigilant in the future, with a watchful eye, to the continuously shifting boundaries between African Americans and whites.

Was I predisposed to marry a "white girl?"

I don't think I ever had a desire to marry someone of one race rather than another. I dated women from a variety of backgrounds before marriage. Although because of my light skin and where I was raised, some may have felt I was destined to marry a white female. When I did, it served as confirmation that my *blackness* was to be questioned. My first girlfriend was African American. We met after I left the public schools and enrolled in a private high school. In junior high there were a couple of girls whom I was interested in but there was no way we could have dated. I was one of three African American men out of nearly 1500 students. Where would we have gone out for a date? There was no place to go at that time where we would not have faced considerable ridicule. School dances were not a possibility. There weren't any formal laws about an interracial couple attending. There were just too many people in the school that I didn't know personally and some would probably have produced very uncomfortable feelings or even situations for us.

There were a couple girls who were interested in me as well when I was in junior high school. A relationship would have had to have been somewhat discrete. Given that there would have been some considerable distances that needed to be traveled in order to have contact, parents would have had to be involved. Some parents did not react favorably to me. Very few mothers gave me a tough time, but the fathers were a very different story and at times seemed quite protective of their daughters.

My wife accepts me for who I am. I do not believe she ever gave any thought to my race when it came to whether or not to have a relationship with me and then to marry. But I knew women prior to my marriage that saw other things about me I wish they had not. Most of my experiences are from the 1980s. I have been married since 1994. I remember once I wanted to date a woman, African American, but I was simply *too white* for her and she refused. My mannerisms were not so much of an issue. But coupled with my physical appearance, I was just too close to her image of a white male. At about the same time, there was an African American woman who really liked me not because I was close to what she perceived white males to be, but because I was quite distant from what she considered many African American men to be, flashy and not proper in behavior.

No, I was not predisposed to marry a "white girl." In fact social forces existed that encouraged me not to straddle the fence or to marry someone of another race. Circumstances allowed me to meet my future wife, to get to know her, fall in love and to eventually marry. I unintentionally went against the grain. But I did not plan to do so. Those same forces that pushed me toward conformity are still with us. The only changes that have occurred are an expansion of situations that allow individuals of different races more opportunity to meet: college campuses, places of employment, public establishments such as restaurants, and more. The underlying racial categories of black versus white are still with us today and crossing the color line still brings scrutiny.

Chapter One

[1] DuBois," The Souls of Black Folk,"1996.
[2] Piper, "Passing for White, Passing for Black,"1992.
[3] Mead, *Mind, Self and Society*, 1932.
[4] Spickard, *Mixed Blood*, 1989.
[5] Gadberry and Doddler, "Educational homogamy in interracial marriages", 1993.
[6] See Brodkin, "How Jews Became White Folks," 2002.
[7] Wilson, *The Declining Significance of* Race, 1978.
[8] Work by Kinder and Mendelberg, "Cracks in American Apartheid", 1995, indicates that segregation was less between African Americans and whites earlier in the 20th century. See Bennett, *Before the Mayflower,* 1982.
[9] Moyer, *Sociopolitical Attitudes*, 1980, pg. 5.
[10] Steinberg, *The Ethnic Myth*, 1989.
[11] Steinberg, *The Ethnic Myth*, 1989.
[12] Brodkin, "How Jews Became White Folks", 2002.
[13] Brodkin, "How Jews Became White Folks," 2002.
[14] Shihadeh and Flynn, "Segregation and Crime." 1996.
[15] Wilson, *The Declining Significance of* Race, 1978.
[16] Moyer, *Sociopolitical Attitudes*, 1980, p.12.
[17] Steinberg, *The Ethnic Myth*, 1989.
[18] Wilson, *When Work Disappears*, 1996.
[19] Wilson, *When Work Disappears*, 1996.
[20] Harris, "Revolutionary Black Nationalism" 2000; Adeleke, "Black Americans and Africa" 1998; Ngozi-Brown, "The Us Organization, Maulana Karenga, and the Conflict with the Black Panther Party," 1997; Martin, "From Negro to Black to African American", 1991.
[21] Tatum, *"Why Are All the Black Kids Sitting Together in the Cafeteria?"* 1997.
[22] Collins, *Black Feminist Thought,* 2000; hooks [sic], *Ain't I a Woman*, 1992
[23] Hurtado, *The Color of Privilege*, 1996, pg. 10.
[24] Hurtado, *The Color of Privilege*, 1996, pg 13.

Chapter Two

[25] Carey, *Black Ice*, 1991.
[26] Steinberg, *The Ethnic Myth*, 1989.
[27] ... the detachment with the highest percentage of Negroes, General Samuel Holden Parson's brigade, was made up primarily of recruits from Connecticut. This was typical: practically no town of any size in that state failed to supply one or more Negroes for the Continental Army. New England, despite its relatively small black population, probably furnished more colored soldiers than any other section. In central Massachusetts in 1777 an observer reported that he ran across no regiment without "a lot of Negroes." The Rhode Island First Regiment enrolled from 225 to 250 colored men.

Outside New England, the state that recruited the largest number of Negroes was Virginia, the total in her land and sea forces perhaps going "beyond the five hundred mark." Quarles, *The Negro in the Making of America*, 1987, pg. 61.

[28] Bennett, *Before the Mayflower*, 1982, pg. 40.

[29] Sutton, *Black, Red, and Revolutionary*, 1997, pg. 210.

[30] Sutton, *Black, Red, and Revolutionary*, 1997.

[31] Davis, *Who is Black?* 1997, pg. 55.

[32] Davis, *Who is Black?* 1997, pg. 160. See Dorr, *Arm in Arm*, 1999, for discussion of Virginia's Racial Integrity Acts.

[33] Gates, *Colored People*, 1995.

[34] Brodkin, "How Jews Became White Folks," 2002, pgs. 41 – 43.

[35] The reader should be aware that there are similarities to post- World War I when there was an increase in animosity between the two groups. The Great War had brought African Americans and whites in closer proximity and "race riots" were the result. There was resurgence in the Ku Klux Klan. Competition for jobs was one factor that fostered unrest. For a good summary see Quarles, *The Negro in the Making of* America, 1987.

[36] Loewen, *Sundown Towns*, 2005, pg. 4.

[37] Dalton, "Failing to See," 2002, pg. 16.

[38] Massey et al, "American Apartheid." 1995, Blumer, "Race Prejudice as a Sense of Group Position," 1958.

Chapter Three

[39] Griffin, "Teaching Region, Learning Humility",2002, pg.5-7.

[40] Lesage et al, *Making a Difference*, 2002.

[41] Collins and Coltraine, Sociology and Marriage in the Family, 1995.

[42] Davis, *Who is Black?* 1997.

[43] Bonacich, "Advanced Capitalism and Black/White Race Relations." 1999.

[44] Omi and Winant, *Racial Formation in the United States*, 1986.

[45] Bennett, *Before the Mayflower*, 1992.

[46] Dickerson et al, "Do Undergraduate College Students Self-Segregate?" 2002.

[47] Massey et al, "American Apartheid," 2002, pg. 322-323.

[48] Steinberg, 1992.

[49] Rawls, "'Race' as an Interaction Order Phenomenon," 2000.

Chapter Four

[50] This area was similar to Levittown and other mass produced housing areas constructed after World War II. Most of the houses were similar to each other with probably a maximum of three bedrooms in each.

[51] Frey, 2002.

[52] Davis, *Who is Black?* 1997.

[53] Loewen, *Sundown Towns*, 2005, writes about a "springtime of race relations between African Americans and whites" between 1865 and 1890. "During those years, African Americans voted, served in Congress, received some spoils from the Republican Party, worked as barbers, railroad firemen, midwives mail carriers, and landowning farmers,

and played other fully human roles in American society…After 1890, as in the South, Jim Crow practices tightened throughout the North. The so-called Progressive movement was for whites only; often its "reforms" removed the last local black leaders from northern city councils in favor of commissioners elected citywide. Northern whites attacked African Americans, verbally and often literally. Segregation swept through public accommodations…" pgs. 29-34.

[54] Piven and Cloward, *Regulating the Poor*, 1971, note that government policies are not always what they may appear to be. That although policies instituted can positively affect the quality of life of a particular group, political parties benefit as well. The reader is asked to entertain the possible connections between the rising number of African American middle class protest groups during the 1960s and 70s and affirmative action policies that benefited the African American middle class and not the mass number of poor African Americans, or white poor. The reader is left to conclude that affirmative action policies not only helped to expand the African American middle class but co-opted or brought quiescence to many of these protests movements given that many of the leaders of these movements, according to Piven and Cloward, were middle and upper class African Americans with college degrees.

[55] Steinberg, *The Ethnic Myth*, 1989.

[56] Davis, *Who is Black?* 1997, pg. 33.

[57] Williamson, *Miscegenation and Mulattoes in the United States*, 1995.

[58] Willie, *Acting Black*, 2003, 36-38.

Chapter 5

[59] Killian, "Race Relations and the Nineties," 1990.

[60] Harris, "Revolutionary Black Nationalism" 2000; Adeleke, "Black Americans and Africa" 1998; Ngozi-Brown, "The Us Organization, Maulana Karenga, and the Conflict with the Black Panther Party," 1997; Martin, "From Negro to Black to African American," 1991.

[61] Anderson, Streetwise, 1990.

[62] Sundstrom, *The Color Line*, 1994.

[63] See Olzak and McEneaney, "Poverty, Segregation, and Race Riots: 1960-1960 to 1993," 1996, for urban unrest.

[64] It should be noted that a second "white flight" is now occurring. Millions of whites are now moving beyond the boundaries of urban and suburban areas to states that are now called the "New Suburbia States." These thirteen states showed an above average growth in the 90s compared to the rest of the nation. The states are: Arizona, Colorado, Washington, North Carolina, South Carolina, Tennessee, Virginia, Delaware, Georgia, Utah, Idaho, Nevada and Oregon. America seems to be separating into 4 different areas. The New Suburbia States where domestic migrants outnumber foreign by five to one, the "melting pot states" (California New York, Texas, Florida, Illinois, New Jersey, New Mexico, Hawaii and Alaska) where the majority of the immigrants reside, the upper Midwest that, similar to the New Suburbia, tends to be majority white, and the south, which is now home to the majority of African Americans in America, slightly more than half. For more detail see work by Frey 2002, 2002, 2003, 2004). For example, although

13 million immigrants, largely from the third world, came to America in the 90s, 73
million people in the 90s moved across state lines to take up a new residence.
[65] Cohn and Fossett, "What Spatial Mismatch?" 1996.
[66] Mead, *Mind, Self and Society*, 1932; Blumer, "Race Prejudice as a Sense of Group
Position," 1958.
[67] Goffman, "On Face-work," 1993.
[68] Wilson, *The Declining Significance of* Race, 1978.
[69] Anderson, *Code of the Street*, 1999.
[70] For a vivid account of some of our nation's high schools see Kozol's, *Savage
Inequalities*, 1992.
[71] Royster, "Race and the Invisible Hand", 2003, pgs. 181 – 189. For what may seem a
contrast in opinion, thus an emphasis more on class than race, see Wilson's now classic
analysis of social problems related to African Americans, *The Declining Significance of
Race*, 1978.
[72] Bobo and Zubrinsky, "Attitudes on Residential Integration," 1996; Jargowsky, "Take
the Money and Run: Economic Segregation in U.S. Metropolitan Areas," 1996.
[73] Dalton, "Failing to See," 2002.
[74] Dickerson et al, "Do Undergraduate College Students Self-Segregate?" 2002.
[75] Fasnacht, "It's Not About Race," 2002.
[76] Bankston, "Majority African American Schools and Social Injustice," 1996.
[77] Logan, Oakley and Stowell, "Segregation in Neighborhoods and Schools,"
2003.
[78] Logan and Oakley, "The Continuing Legacy of the Brown Decision," 2004.
[79] Ogbu, *Black American Students in an American Suburb*, 2003.
[80] Mead, *Mind, Self and* Society, 1932.
[81]Shapiro, *The Hidden Cost of Being African* American, 2004, pgs. 140-142.
[82] Blumer, "Race Prejudice as a Sense of Group Position," 1958.
[83] Goffman, "On Face-work", 1993; Blumer, "Race Prejudice as a Sense of Group
Position," 1958.

Chapter Six

[84] Again, issues of race are important here. Although African Americans as a group are
more socially conservative than whites, African American men do more housework than
white males, according to the text by Collins and Coltrane, *Sociology of Marriage and
the Family*, 1995. Thus, African American households are more traditional only in held
values but in actual household participation as well as working outside the house, there
are significant differences between men and women that are influenced by race.
[85] Dickerson et al, "Do Undergraduate College Students Self-Segregate?" 2002.
[86] Collins, *Black Feminist Thought*, 2000.

Chapter Seven

[87] See Chakraborti and Garland eds., *Rural Racism*, 2004, for an informative discussion
and account of racism in rural areas.

[88] See Carl Rowan's *Dream Makers, Dream* Breakers, on Thurgood Marshall to understand and experience more about the social climate in the South during the 1950s and 60s.

[89] Surprisingly not many studies have been done on intimacy between African Americans or whites and they include: Davis, "Intermarriage in Caste Societies", 1941; Merton, 1941; Bernard, "Note on Educational Homogamy in Negro-white and white-Negro Marriages, 1960; Porterfield, 1982; Spickard, 1989; Tucker and Mitchell-Kernan, 1990; Kouri and Lasswell, 1993; Gadberry and Doddler, 1993; Williamson, 1995. Perhaps this reflects an emphasis that began in the 1960s to place more emphasis on same-race couples rather than inter-race couples as a result of the Black Power movement which criticized previous assimilation and integration social movements Mills, *The Racial Contract*, 1999.

[90] Kouri and Lasswell, "Black-white Marriages", 1993, as well as Porterfield, "Black-American Intermarriage in the United States", both on non-college populations, showed that the primary determinants of interracial dating were meeting in integrated settings and holding similar values.

[91] The names of those interviewed have been changed.

[92] Merton, "Intermarriage and the Social Structure," 1941.

[93] DuBois, "The Souls of Black Folk," 1996, Anderson, Streetwise, 1990.

[94] Brown, *Prejudice*, 1995.

[95] Kouri and Lasswell, "Black-white Marriages," 1993.

[96] It is interesting to note that the movement to recognize biracial children was based on raising the self-esteem of these children. Williams, *New People: Miscegnation and Mulattoes in the United States*, 2005.

[97] McIntosh, "White Privilege: Unpacking the Invisible Knapsack," 2002.

[98] Blumer, "Race Prejudice as a Sense of Group Position," 1958

[99] Omi and Winant, *Racial Formation in the United* States, 1986, Redfield et al, "Memorandum for the Study of Acculturation," 1936.

[100] Willie, 1975; Tajfel and Turner, 1986; Tatum, 1997.

[101] Gordon, *Assililation in American Life*, 1964 p56.

[102] Gordon, *Assililation in American Life*, 1964 p62.

[103] Collins and Coltrane, *Sociology of Marriage and the Family*, 1995.

[104] Gavazzi, 2000 Although the percentage of students at River University who were from the surrounding communities (rural areas) was near 40%, I found more white females, higher than the 40%, who dated interracially, were from rural areas rather than suburban.

[105] Lane, Daugherty, "Correlates of Social Alienation among College Students," 1999.

[106] There probably will be objection to the implication here that predominantly white fraternities and sororities are not diverse. One of the interesting discussions that can occur in a classroom is how one is to define diversity, especially how many members of a minority group present in a predominantly white social organization constitutes diversity. For some, to have one or two members of a minority group in an organization means diversity has been achieved. For others, and few espouse this position, to diversify may mean something that is very inflated, perhaps trying to reach a level where, for example, 30% of the members would be African American.

[107] Wechsler, Dowdall, Maenner, "Changes in Binge Drinking an Related Problems among American College Students between 1993 and 1997." 1998.

[108] Hamilton 1999; Schalken et al, "Sorority Women's Body Size Perceptions and Their Weight-Related Attitudes and Behavior," 1997.

[109] Campbell, 1988

[110] Lane and Dougherty, "Correlates of Social Alienation among College Students." 1999. It is also possible that my sample size was not large enough to consider the fact that River had an over representation of students from a rural background.

[111] Merton and Rossi, "Contributions to the Theory of Reference Group Behavior," 1968

[112] Monahan, "Interracial Marriage in the United States: Some Data on Upstate New York," 1971; Blau, "A Macrostructural Theory of Social Structure," 1977; Blau, Blum and Schwartz, "Heterogeneity and Intermarriage," 1982.

[113] Monahan, "Interracial Marriage in the United States: Some Data on Upstate New York," 1971

[114] Monahan, "Interracial Marriage in the United States: Some Data on Upstate New York," 1971; Blau, "A Macrostructural Theory of Social Structure," 1977; Blau, Blum and Schwartz, "Heterogeneity and Intermarriage," 1982.

[115] Hochschild, "American Racial and Ethnic Politics in the 21st Century," 1998.

[116] Hochschild, "American Racial and Ethnic Politics in the 21st Century," 1998.

[117] hooks [sic], *Ain't I a Woman?*, 1992; Zinn, Dill. "Theorizing Difference from Multicultural Feminsim", 1996.

[118] Davis, "Intermarriage in Caste Societies," 1941; Merton, Intermarriage and the Social Structure: Fact and Theory," 1941.

[119] Bernard, "Note on Educational Homogamy in Negro-white and white-Negro Marriages, 1960; Porterfield, 1982.

[120] Collins and Coltraine, *Sociology of Marriage and the Family*, 1995.

Chapter 8

[121] I recognize that there are multiple feminisms, not simply "black" or "white" feminism.

[122] Higginbotham and Weber, "Moving Up with Kin and Community", 2001, pgs. 159-160. In addition to both of my parents working, almost all of my father's friends, who were members in his club, were dual-income families. Both the husband and wife worked.

[123] Higginbotham and Weber, "Moving Up with Kin and Community," 2001, pgs. 161.

[124] Collins, *Black Feminist Thought*, 2000.

[125] Baylor, "Black and Gay Identity Selection on College Campuses," 2002.

[126] Moore, "Race, Gender and Intimacy on a College Campus," 2002.

[127] Davis, *Women, Race, and Class*, 1981.

[128] Dill, "Our Mothers' Grief: Racial-Ethnic Women and the Maintenance of Families," 2001, pg. 272

[129] hooks [sic], "Black and Female: Reflections on Graduate School," 2003, pg. 409

[130] Higginbotham and Weber, "Moving Up with Kin and Community," 2001,, pg. 162.

[131] Collins 19909, 52

[132] Higginbotham and Weber, "Moving Up with Kin and Community," 2001,, 2001, pg. 163

Conclusion

[133] Johnson, "The Autobiography of an Ex-Colored Man," 1969. pgs. 504-509.
[134] See Mary Water's article"Optional Ethnicities: For White's Only?" on "optional ethnicities" for whites. Also see Yancey's book, *Who is White? Latinos, Asians, and the New Black/Nonblack Divide,* for discussion about the continued racial demarcation between African Americans and whites.

References

Adeleke, Tunde. "Black Americans and Africa: A Critique of the Pan-Africa and Identity Paradigms," *The International Journal of African Historical Studies* 31, no. 3(1998): 505-536.

Adorno, T. W., E. Frenkel-Brunswick, D.J. Levinson and R. N. Sanford. *The Authoritarian Personality*. New York: Harper and Row, 1950.

Allport, Gordon W. *The Nature of Prejudice*. Boston, Mass: Beacon, 1954.

Anderson, Elijah. *Streetwise*. Chicago: University of Chicago Press, 1990.

_____ *Code of the Street: Decency, Violence, and the Moral Life of the Inner City*. New York: W. W. Norton and Co, 1999.

Bankston III, Carl. "Majority African American Schools and Social Injustice: The Influence of De Facto Segregation on Academic Achievement," *Social Forces*, 75, no. 2(1996) 535-555.

Baylor, Tim. "Black and Gay Identity Selection on College Campuses: Master and Subordinate Status Strain and Conflict." In *The Quality and Quantity of Contact: African Americans and Whites on College Campuses*, edited by Robert M. Moore III, 123-142. Lanham: University Press of America, 2002.

Bennett, Lerone. *Before the Mayflower: A History of Black America*. New York: Penguin, 1982.

Bernard, J. "Note on Educational Homogamy in Negro-white and white-Negro Marriages," *Journal of Marriage and the Family* 28 (1960)274-276.

Blau, Peter M. "A Macrostructural Theory of Social Structure," *American Journal of Sociology* 83, no.1 (1977): 26-54.

Blau, Peter M., T.C. Blum, and J. E. Schwartz. "Heterogeneity and Intermarriage," *American Sociological Review* 47(1982): 45-62.

Blumer, H. "Race Prejudice as a Sense of Group Position," *Pacific Sociological Review* 1, no. 1(1958): 3-7.

Bobo, Lawrence D. "Prejudice as Group Position: Microfoundations of a Sociological Approach to Racism and Race Relations," *Journal of Social Issues* 55, no. 3(1999): 445-472.

Bobo, Lawrence D. and V. L. Hutchings. "Perceptions of racial groups competition: extending Blumer's theory of group position to a multiracial social context," *American Sociological Review* 61(1996): 951-972.

Bobo, Lawrence D. and C. L. Zubrinsky. "Attitudes on Residential   Integration: Perceived Status Differences, Mere In-group Preference, or Racial Prejudice?," *Social Forces* 74, no.3 (1996): 883-909.

Bonacich, Edna. "Advanced Capitalism and Black/White Race Relations in the United States: A Split Labor Market Interpretation." In *Rethinking the Color Line: Readings in Race and Ethnicity*, edited by C. A. Gallagher, 206 – 221. Mountain View, Ca: Mayfield Publishing. 1999.

Brodkin, Karen. "How Jews Became White Folks." In *White Privilege: Essential Readings on the Other Side of Racism*, edited by Paula S. Rothenberg, 35-48. Worth Publishers: New York: 2002.

Brown, Rupert. *Prejudice: It's Social Psychology*. Cambridge: Blackwell, 1995.

Cary, Lorene. *Black Ice*. New York: Vintage Books, 1991.

Chakraborti, Neil and Jon Garland. ed. *Rural Racism*. Devon, England: William Publishing, 2004.

Cohn, Samuel and Mark Fossett. "What spatial Mismatch? The proximity of Blacks to employment in Boston and Houston," *Social Forces* 75, no. 2 (1996): 557-573.

Collins, Patricia Hill. *Black Feminist Thought: Knowledge, Consciousness, and the Politics of Empowerment*, 2nd edition. New York: Routledge, 2000.

Collins, Randall and Scott Coltrane. *Sociology of Marriage and the Family*. Chicago: Nelson - Hall, 1995, chapter 9.

Cross Jr., William E. "The Psychology of Nigrescence: Revising the Cross Model," In *Handbook of Multicultural Counseling* , edited by Joseph G. Ponterotto, J. Manuel

Casas, Lisa A. Suzuki and Charlene M. Alexander, 93-122. Thousand Oaks, CA: Sage, 1995.

Dalton, Harlon, "Failing to See." In *White Privilege: Essential Readings on the Other Side of Racism* , edited by Paula S. Rothenberg, 14-18. New York: Worth Pulbishers, 2002.

Davis, Angela Y. *Women, Race and Class*. New York: Vintage Books, 1981.

Davis, F. James. *Who is Black? One nation's definition*. University Park, PA: Penn State University, 1997.

Davis, Kingsley "Intermarriage in Caste Societies," *American Anthropologist* 43 (1941): 376-395.

Dickerson, Bette J., Kianda Bell, Kathryn Lasso, and Tiffany Waits. "Do Undergraduate College Students Self-Segregate?,"In *The Quality and Quantity of Contact: African Americans and Whites on College Campuses* , edited by Robert M. Moore III, 254-286. Lanham: University Press of America, 2002.

Dill, Bonnie Thornton. "Our Mothers' Grief: Racial-Ethnic Women and the Maintenance of Families." In *Race, Class and Gender* , edited by M. L. Andersen and Patricia Hill Collins, 268-88. Belmont, CA: Wadsworth, 2001.

Dorr, Lisa Lundquist. "Arm in Arm: Gender, Eugenics, and Virginia's Racial Integrity Acts of the 1920s," *Journal of Women's History* 11, no.1(1999): 143-166.

DuBois, W. E. B. *The Philadelphia Negro*. Millwood, NY: Kraus-Thomson Organization Ltd., 1973.

_____ "The Souls of Black Folks." In *Oxford W. E. B. DuBois Reader* , edited by Eric J. Sundquist, 97-241, New York: Oxford University Press, 1996.

Fasnacht, Natalie. "'It's Not About Race:' Making Whiteness Visible in the Interpretation of Rap Music." In *The Quality and Quantity of Contact: African Americans and Whites on College Campuses* , edited by Robert M. Moore III, 48-79. Lanham: University Press of America, 2002.

Festinger, Leon. *A Theory of Cognitive Dissonance*. Stanford: Stanford Univ. Press, 1957.

Forman, Tyrone A. "Color-blind Racism and Racial Indifference: The Role of Racial Apathy in Facilitating Enduring Inequalities." In *The Changing Terrain of Race and Ethnicity* , edited by Maria Krysan and Amanda E. Lewis, 43-67. New York: Russell Sage Foundation, 2004.

Frankenburg, Ruth. *White Women Race Matters: The Social Construction of Whiteness*. Minneapolis: University of Minnesota Press, 1993.

References

Frey, William H. "Metro Magnets for Minorities and Whites: Melting Pots, the New Sunbelt, and the Heartland" Population Studies Center Report No. 02-496. Institute for Social Research: University of Michigan, 2002.

_____ "Migration Swings," *American Demographics* 24, no.2 (2002): 18-21.

_____ "Metropolitan Magnets for International and Domestic Migrants" Brookings Census 2000 Series. Washington D.C: Brookings Institution Center on Urban and Metropolitan Policy, October 2003.

_____ "The New Great Migration: Black Americans 'Return to the South,' 1965 – 2000" Brookings Census 2000 Series. Washington D.C: Brookings Institution Center on Urban and Metropolitan Policy, May 2004.

Gadberry, James H. and Richard A. Doddler. "Educational Homogamy in   Interracial Marriages: An Update," *Journal of Social Behavior and Personality* 8 (1993): 155-163.

Gallagher, Charles A. "Would but Don't: Reconciling Expressed Willingness to Intergroup Marriage with National Trends." In *The Quality and Quantity of Contact: African Americans and Whites on College Campuses*, edited by Robert M. Moore III, 240-253. Lanham: University Press of America, 2002.

Gates Jr., Henry Louis. *Colored People: A Memoir*. New York: Vintage, 1995.

Goffman, Erving. "On Face-work." In *Social Theory: The Multicultural and Classic Readin*, edited by Charles Lemert, 199-204. Boulder, CO: Westview Press, 1993.

Griffin, Larry. "Teaching Region, Learning Humility." In *The Quality and Quantity of Contact: African Americans and Whites on College Campuses*, edited by Robert M. Moore III, 1-17. Lanham: University Press of America, 2002.

Haizlip, Shirlee. *The Sweeter the Juice: A Family Memoir in Black and White*. New York: Simon and Schuster, 1995.

Helms, Janet E. "An Update of Helms' White and People of Color Racial Identity Models." In *Handbook of Multicultural Counseling*, edited by Joseph g. Ponterotto, J. Manuel Casas, Lisa A. Suzuki and Charlene M. Alexander, 181-198. Thousand Oaks, CA: Sage, 1995.

Harris, Jessica C. "Revolutionary Black Nationalism: The Black Panther Party," *Journal of Negro History* 85, no.3(2000): 162-174.

Higginbotham, E. and L. Weber."Moving up with Kin and Community." In *Race, Class and Gender* , edited by M. L. Andersen and Patricia Hill Collins,156-167. Belmont, Ca: Wadsworth, 2001.

Hirschman, C. Alba, R. and R. Farley. 2000. "The Meaning and Measurement of Race in the U.S. Census: Glimpses into the Future," Demography. Vol 37, 381-393.

Hochschild. Jennifer L. "American Racial and Ethnic Politics in the 21st Century: A Cautious Look Ahead," *The Brookings Review* 16, no 2, (1998): 43-46.

hooks, bell [sic]. "Black and Female: Reflections on Graduate School." In *Reconstructing Gender: A Multicultural Anthology* , edited by Estelle Disch, 405-410. New York: McGraw Hill, 2003

_____ *Ain't I a Woman: Black Women and Feminism*. Boston: South End Press, 1992.

_____ *Black Looks: Race and Representation*. Boston: South End Press, 1992.

Hughes, Michael and Melvin E. Thomas. "The Continuing Significance of Race Revisited: A Study of Race, Class, and Quality of Life in America, 1972 to 1996," *American Sociological Review* 63, no. 6(1998): 785-795.

Hurtado, Aida. *The Color of Privilege*. Ann Arbor: The University of Michigan Press, 1996.

Iceland, John. "Urban Labor Markets and Individual Transitions Out of Poverty." *Demography* 34, no.3(1997): 429-441.

Jargowsky, Paul A. "Take the Money and Run: Economic Segregation in U.S. Metropolitan Areas," *American Sociological Review*. 61, no.6 (1996): 984-998.

Johnson, James Weldon. "The Autobiography of an ex-colored man." In *Three Negro Classics: Up from Sllavery. The Souls of Black Folk. The Autobiography of an Ex-colored Man*, 391-511. New York: Discus Books, 1969

Killian, Lewis M. "Race Relations and the Nineties: Where are the Dreams of the Sixties?," *Social Forces* 69, no.1(1990): 1-13.

Kinder, Donald R. and Tali Mendelberg. "Cracks in American Apartheid: The Political Impact of Prejudice among Desegregated Whites," *Journal of Politics* 57, no.2 (1995):402-424.

Kouri, K. M. and M. Lasswell. 1993. "Black-white marriages: social change and intergenerational mobility," *Marriage and Family Review* 19 #3-4. pp. 241-

Kozol, Jonathan. *Savage Inequalities: Children in America's Schools*. New York: Harper Perennial, 1992.

Kwong, Peter. *The New Chinatown*. New York: Noonday Press, 1987.

Lane, E. J. and T. K. Dougherty. "Correlates of social alienation   among college students," *College Student Journal* 33, no.1 (1999):7-9.

Lesage, Julia, Abbie L. Ferber, Storrs, Debbie Storrs, and Donna Wong. *Making a Difference: University Students of Color Speak Out*. New York: Rowan and Littlefield, 2002.

Lewis, David Levering. *When Harlem was in Vogue*. New York: Penguin Books, 1997.

Lewis, John and Michael D'Orso. *Walking with the Wind: A Memoir of the Movement*. New York: Simon and Schuster. 1997.

Loewen, James W. *Sundown Towns: A Hidden Dimension of American Racism*. New York: The New Press, 2005.

Logan, John R. and Deirdre Oakley. 2004. "The Continuing Legacy of the Brown Decision: Court Action and School Segregation, 1960-2000". Lewis Mumford Center for Comparative Urban and Regional Research, University of Albany, Jan. 28, 2004.

Logan, John R., Deirdre Oakley and Jacob Stowell. "Segregation in Neighborhoods and Schools: Impacts on Minority Children in the Boston Region." Lewis Mumford Center for Comparative Urban and Regional Research, University of Albany, Sept 1 2003.

Martin, B. L. "From Negro to Black to African American: The Power of Names and Naming," *Political Science Quarterly* 106, no. 1,(1991) 83-107.

Massey, Douglas S., N.A. Denton and I. Luckey. "American Apartheid: Segregation and the Making of the Underclass," *The Social Service Review* 69(1995):773.

McIntosh, Peggy. "White Privilege: Unpacking the Invisible Knapsack." In *White Privilege: Essential Readings on the Other Side of Racism* , edited by Paula S. Rothenberg, 97-102. Worth Publishers: New York, 2002.

Mead, George. Herbert. *Mind, Self and Society from the Standpoint of a Social Behaviorist*, ed. Charles W. Morris. Chicago: University of Chicago, 1932.

Merton, Robert K. "Intermarriage and the Social Structure: Fact and Theory," *Psychiatry* 4(1941): 361-374.

Merton, Robert K. and Alice Kitt Rossi. "Contributions to the Theory of Reference Group Behavior." In *Readings in Reference Group Theory and Research, ed.* Herbert Hyman and Eleanor Singer. London: Free Press, 1968.

Mills, Charles W. *The Racial Contract*. Ithaca: Cornell University, 1999.

Monahan, Thomas P. "Interracial Marriage in the United States: Some Data on Upstate New York," *International Journal of Sociology of the Family* 1, special issue(1971): 49-58.

Moore III, R. M. 2002. "Race, Gender and Intimacy on a College Campus." In The Quality and Quantity of Contact: African Americans and Whites on College Campuses. Ed. Robert M. Moore III. New York: University Press of America.

Moyer, Kathleen J. "Sociopolitical Attitudes and Political Behavior in a Working Class Suburb." Phd. Diss, Bryn Mawr College, 1979.

Nelson, Jr., W. "Black Political Consciousness and Empowerment: The 20th Century Cognitive Basis of African American Politics." In *Black Identity in the 20th Century: Expressions of the US and UK African Diaspora* , edited by Mark Christian, chapter 4. London: Hansib, 2002

Newcomb, Theodore M., Kathryn E. Koenig, Richard Flacks and Donald P. Warwick. *Persistence and Change: Bennington College and its students after twenty-five years*. New York: Wiley, 1967.

Ngozi-Brown, Scot. "The Us Organization, Maulana Karenga, and the Conflict with the Black Panther Party: A Critique of Sectarian Influences on Historical Discourses," *Journal of Black Studies* 28, no.2(1997): 157-170.

Ogbu, John U. *Black American Students in an Affluent Suburb: A Study of Academic Disengagement*. Mahwah, New Jersey: L. Erlbaum Associates, 2003.

Olzak, S., S. Shanahan and E. II. McEneaney. "Poverty, segregation and Race Riots: 1960 to 1993," *American Sociology Review* 61, no. 4 (1996):590-613.

Omi, Michael and Howard Winant *Racial Formation in the United States: From the 1960s to the 1980s*. New York: Routledge and Kegan Paul, 1986.

Piper, Adrian. "Passing for White, Passing for Black," *Transition* 58 (1992): 4-32.

Piven, Frances Fox and Richard A. Cloward. *Regulatin the Poor: The Functions of Public Welfare*. New York: Vintage, 1971.

Porterfield, Ernest. "Black-American Intermarriage in the United States," *Marriage and Family Review* 5, no.(1982): 17-34.

Quadagno, Jill. *The Color of Welfare: How Racism Undermined the War on Poverty*. New York: Oxford University Press, 1994.

Quarles, Benjamin. *The Negro in the Making of America*. New York: Simon and Schuster, 1987.

Ramirez, Deborah. "Multicultural Empowerment: It's Not Just Black and White Anymore," *Stanford Law Review* 47, no. 5(1995) 957-992.

Rawls, Anne Warfield. "'Race' as an Interaction Order Phenomenon: W.E.B. DuBois' 'Double Consciousness' Thesis Revisited," *Sociological Theory* 18, no. 2 (2000): 241-274.

Redfield, L. and M. Herskovits. "Memorandum for the study of Acculturation," *American Anthropologist* 38, no.1 (1936).

Reuter, E. B. "The Personality of Mixed Bloods." In *Personality and the Social Group* , edited by Ernest W. Burgess, 55-63. Freeport, NY: Libraries Press, 1969.

Roberts, S. "In Manhattan, Poor Make 2 Cents for Every Dollar to Rich," *New York Times*, Sept 4, 2005.

Rockquemore, Kerry Ann and David L. Brunsma. *Beyond Black: Biracial Identity in America*. Thousand Oaks: Sage, 2002.

Ross, Lee and Richard E. Nisbett. *The Person and the Situation: Perspectives of Social Psychology*. New York: McGraw-Hill, 1991.

Royster, Dee A. *Race and the Invisible Hand: How white networks exclude black men from blue-collar jobs*. Berkeley: University of California Press, 2003.

Rowan, Carl T. *Dream Makers, Dream Breakers: The World of Justice Thurgood Marshall*. New York: Little, Brown and Co., 1993.

Schaefer, Richard T. "Education and prejudice: unraveling the relationship," The Sociological Quarterly 37, Winter (1996): 1-16.

Schulken, E. D., Pinciaro, P. J., and R. G. Sawyer. "Sorority Women's body size Perceptions and Their Weight-related Attitudes and Behavior," *Journal of American College Health* 46, September(1997): 69-74.

Shapiro, Thomas M. *The Hidden Cost of being African American: How wealth perpetuates inequality*. New York: Oxford University Press, 2004.

Sherif, Muzafer, O.J. Harvey, B. Jack White, William R.Hood and Carolyn W. Sherif. *Intergroup Conflict and Cooperation: The Robbers Cave Experiment*. (Norman: University of Oklahoma Book Exchange, 1961.

Shihadeh, Edward S. and Nicole Flynn. "Segregation and Crime: The Effects of Black Social Isolation on the Rates of Black Urban Violence," *Social Forces* 74, no.4(1996): 1325-1352.

Sidanius, Jim and Felicia Pratto. "Racism and Support of Free-Market Capitalism: A Cross-Cultural Analysis," *Political Psychology* 14, no. 3(1993): 381-401.

Sidanius, Jim, Felicia Pratto and M. Mitchell. "In-group Identification, Social Dominance Orientation, and Differential Intergroup Social Allocation," *Journal of Social Psychology* 134 no. 2(1994): 151-168.

Sidanius, Jim, Felicia Pratto and J. L. Rabinowitz. "Gender, Ethnic Status, and Ideological Asymmetry: a Social Dominance Interpretation," *Journal of Cross-Cultural Psychology* 25, no. 2(1994): 194-217.

Spickard, Paul R. *Mixed blood: Intermarriage and Ethnic Identity in Twentieth-Century America.* Madison: University of Wisconsin Press, 1989.

Staples, Robert. *The Black Family: Essays and Studies, 6ᵗʰ ed.* Belmont, CA: Wadsworth Pub Co., 1999.

Steinberg, Stephen. *The Ethnic Myth: Race, Ethnicity, and Class in America.* Boston: Beacon Press, 1989.

_____ *Turning Back: The Retreat from Racial Justice in American Thought and Policy.* Boston: Beacon Press, 2001.

Sundstrom, William A. "The Color Line: Racial Norms and Discrimination in Urban Labor Markets, 1910-1950," *The Journal of Economic History* 54, no. 2 (1994): 382-396.

Sutton, Karen E. "Black, Red and Revolutionary: Free African Americans of Lancaster and Northumberland Counties, Virginia in the Era of the American Revolution." Master's Project, Master of Arts, History, University of Maryland, 1997.

Tajfel, H. and J. C. Turner. "The social identity theory of intergroup behavior," In *Psychology of Intergroup Relations* Stephen Worchel and William G. Austin, 7-24. Chicago: Nelson-Hall, 1986.

Tatum, Beverly D. "Why Are All the Black kids Sitting Together in the Cafeteria?And Other Conversations About Race" New York: Basic, 1997, 75-90.

Tucker, M. Belinda and Claudia Mitchell-Kernan. "New Trends in Black American Interracial Marriage: The Social Structural Context," *Journal of Marriage and Family* 52, February(1990): 209-218.

U.S. Census. Table 1. Race of Wife by Race of Husband: 1960, 1970, 1980, 1991 and 1992. Internet Release date: 06/10/98. http://www.census.gov/population/socdemo/race/interractab1.txt (Accessed 9/3/06).

U.S. Census. *1990 Census Database C90STF3A Summary Level State-County.*

Stats Canada. 2005. *Visible minority population, by provinces and territories (2001 Census)* table, Stats Canada. (Accessed via internet, October 3, 2005)

Water, Mary. "Optional Ethnicities: For Whites Only?" In *Rethinking the Color Line: Readings in Race and Ethnicity*, edited by Charles A. Gallagher, 95-108. Mountain View, Ca: Mayfield Publishing, 2004.

Wechsler, H., Dowell, G. W. and G. Maemer. "Changes in Binge Drinking and Related Problems Among American College Students between 1993 and 1997: Results of the Harvard School of Public Health Alcohol Study," *Journal of American College Health*, 47, no. 2(1998):57-68.

Wilds, Deborah J. "Minorities in Higher Education 1999-2000: Seventeenth Annual Status Report." American Council of Education: Washington D.C., 2000.

Williams, Kim M. "Multiracialism and the civil rights future." *Daedalus*, 134, no. 1 (2005)

Williamson, Joel. *New People: Miscegenation and Mulattoes in the United States*. Baton Rouge: Louisiana State University Press, 1995.

Willie, Charles V. *Oreo: A Perspective on Race and Marginal Men and Women*. Wakefield, Mass.: Parameter Press, 1975.

Willie, Sarah Susannah. *Acting Black: College Identity, and the Performance of Race*. New York: Routledge, 2003.

Wilson, William Julius. *The Declining Significance of Race: Blacks and Changing American Institutions*. Chicago: University of Chicago Press, 1978.

_____ *When Work Disappears*. New York: Vintage Books, 1996.

Yancey, George. *Who is White? Latinos, Asians, and the New Black/Nonblack Divide*. Boulder: Lynne Rienner Publishers, 2003.

Zinn, Maxine B. and Bonnie T. Dill.. "Theorizing Difference from Multicultural Feminism." Feminist Studies 22, Summer(1996): 321-31.

About the Author

Robert M. Moore III is Associate Professor of Sociology and Coordinator of the African American Studies program at Frostburg State University. Actively involved in the Southern Sociological Society, he is a member of the program committee and the past chair of the committee on race and ethnic minorities. Dr. Moore also served one term as president of the Pennsylvania Sociological Society. He recently received teaching and service awards from the university and was nominated for a State of Maryland Higher Education Regents' award for outstanding teaching. As a Visiting Associate Professor at the University of Waterloo while on sabbatical, he taught a course on race to Canadian students. He has edited three books each a collection of articles, *The Hidden America: Social Problems in Rural America for the Twenty-first Century*; *The Quality and Quantity of Contact: African Americans and Whites on College Campuses*; *African Americans and Whites: Changing Relationships on College Campuses*. He received his Ph.D. in Social Psychology from Temple University.

Index